# Myths of Power
*Anniversary Edition*

# Myths of Power
## A Marxist Study of the Brontës

Terry Eagleton
*Professor of Cultural Theory, Manchester University*

Featuring new Introduction to the Anniversary Edition

First published 2005 by
PALGRAVE MACMILLAN
Houndmills, Basingstoke, Hampshire RG21 6XS and
175 Fifth Avenue, New York, N. Y. 10010
Companies and representatives throughout the world

PALGRAVE MACMILLAN is the global academic imprint of the Palgrave Macmillan division of St. Martin's Press, LLC and of Palgrave Macmillan Ltd. Macmillan® is a registered trademark in the United States, United Kingdom and other countries. Palgrave is a registered trademark in the European Union and other countries.

ISBN-13: 978-1–4039–4697–3 hardback
ISBN-10: 1–4039–4697–3 hardback
ISBN-13: 978-1–4039–4698–0 paperback
ISBN-10: 1–4039–4698–1 paperback

This book is printed on paper suitable for recycling and made from fully managed and sustained forest sources.

A catalogue record for this book is available from the British Library.

Library of Congress Cataloging-in-Publication Data
Eagleton, Terry, 1943–
    Myths of Power : a Marxist study of the Brontës / Terry Eagleton. –
–Anniversary ed.
        p. cm
    Includes bibliographical references and index.
    ISBN 1–4039–4697–3 (cloth) — ISBN 1–4039–4698–1 (pbk.)
        1. Brontè, Charlotte, 1816–1855—Criticism and interpretation.
    2. Brontè, Emily, 1818–1848—Criticism and interpretation. 3. Brontè,
    Anne, 1820–1849—Criticism and interpretation. 4 Literature and
    society—England—History—19th century. 5. Women and literature–
    –England—History—19th century. 6. English fiction—19th century–
    –History and criticism. 7. Power (Social sciences) in literature. 8. Marxist
    criticism. 9. Brontè family. I. Title.

PR4169.E2 2005
823'.809—dc22

                                                    2004061203

10   9   8   7   6   5   4   3   2   1
14  13  12  11  10  09  08  07  06  05

Printed and bound in Great Britain by
Antony Rowe Ltd, Chippenham and Eastbourne

For

DOMINIC and DANIEL
and the working-class movement
of West Yorkshire

# Contents

# Acknowledgements

This book began as an article on Charlotte Brontë which appeared in the *Critical Quarterly*, and I should like to thank the editors of that journal for their permission to reprint parts of the original piece in modified form. The article was encouragingly commented on by Ian Gregor, Bernard Sharratt, Stan Smith and Charles Swann; and I must thank them for lending me the impetus to develop it into a book. My wife Rosemary read and valuably criticised the manuscript, as did five of my friends and students: Francis Barker, Tom Birmingham, Honora Hickey, Alan Wall and George Wotton. I am deeply grateful to them all for their close, continuous involvement in the writing of the book; and I must particularly thank Francis Barker, who was kind enough to check the note references. I am also much indebted to Katherine Turner, Clive Field, and my colleague A. F. Thompson, who gave me valuable help with historical research.

All quotations from the works of the Brontës and from Mrs Gaskell's *Life of Charlotte Brontë* have been taken from the Haworth edition of *The Life and Works of Charlotte Brontë and her Sisters*, edited by Mrs H. Ward and C. K. Shorter (London, 1899–1900).

T.E.

*Wadham College,*
*Oxford*
*April 1974*

A*

# Introduction to the Anniversary Edition

The Brontës, I suppose, could be described as late Romantic writers, which is more than just a comment on chronology. They emerged as authors towards the end of the great Romantic epoch around the turn of the nineteenth century, and towards the beginning of industrial capitalist England. As such, they were transitional figures, flourishing as they did in the overlap between an era of high Romantic, revolutionary drama, and the birth of a new, crisis-racked form of industrial society. It was a society which had its origin in the factories and cotton mills of the Brontës' own region (the north of England), but was eventually to spread itself across the planet.

The sisters, then, were quite literally writing at the source of global industrial society. The Industrial Revolution began on their doorstep, almost within sight of their parsonage windows. One of their novels, Charlotte's *Shirley*, takes industrial Yorkshire as its subject-matter. To be provincial writers at this particular time and place, ironically, was to spring from a setting of world-historical significance. There were few more resonant names in the mid-nineteenth century, familiar to many a far-flung sector of the world, than Bradford and Manchester, Leeds and Liverpool. Yet artists are not just the offspring of their contemporary moment. It is not always simple to say to which period a writer belongs. They may be survivors from a previous era, hangovers from a glorious past. Or they may be harbingers of a dimly discernible future. A good many modernist artists of the early twentieth century combined the two, turning backwards to a more primitive, archaic or organic civilisation in order to glimpse within it the lineaments of the new. It is a complex timeloop relevant to the narrative of *Wuthering Heights*.

Are Heathcliff and Catherine Romantic, archaic throwbacks or revolutionary precursors? Or are they both at the same time?
For the Brontë sisters, being late Romantics meant belonging to
at least two eras at once. They had been brought up by their autocratic Tory father on a diet of heroic deeds and mythological
figures, taught to venerate the Duke of Wellington and to admire
whatever was high-spirited and noble-minded. All this reflected the
revolutions and counter-revolutions of the Romantic period, with
its flamboyance and panache. It was one of those rare stretches of
time in which one could sense history literally in the making, as
from Paris to Boston the ground shifted tumultuously beneath men
and women's feet and a whole new revolutionary sensibility was
brought to birth. It is the age of Blake and Robespierre, Hegel and
Jefferson, of startling new creations all the way from the poetry of
Byron and Shelley to the American Constitution and the philosophy of Kant. It is also a post-Enlightenment period, in which the
conception of men and women as rational, restricted animals is
yielding to a view of them as passionate, desirous creatures whose
true home is infinity. The creative imagination is on the loose,
forming strange alliances with revolutionary politics.
To emerge, like the sisters, in the twilight of this epoch meant
among other things to be nostalgic for a lost greatness. Like the
novelist Stendhal, chronicler of the post-Napoleonic period in
France, a precious glory has faded, as the poetics of insurrection
and the melodrama of military conquest give way to the dull prose
of everyday middle-class life. The creative or utopian imagination
now runs headlong into conflict with the harsh disciplines of the
world's first industrial nation. There is a microcosm of this shift in
the way that the sisters had to leave behind a childhood full of myth
and romance in order to buckle down to the austere, soul-
destroying regime of the Victorian governess.
At the same time, there was a certain satisfaction to be reaped for
the Brontës from the fact that the more disruptive currents of revolution had been stemmed, and order and hierarchy restored. In
early nineteenth-century England, a current of militant working-
class discontent was violently quelled by a brutally authoritarian
police state. It would be revived in the sisters' own lifetime, in the
shape of the mass working-class movement of Chartism. As both
free-spirited rebels and Romantic conservatives, the Brontës sym-

pathised with such dissent and feared it, resented authority and admired it. It is a classic lower-middle-class ambiguity, as this study tries to show. In some ways, the sisters can be ranked among those strange, oxymoron beasts, radical conservatives; and as such they belong to a distinguished literary lineage, all the way from John Ruskin and Joseph Conrad to T. S. Eliot and D. H. Lawrence.

The Brontës, then, inherit both the turbulent and traditionalist aspects of the age which precedes them. As I try to show, they are both rebels and reactionaries, pious conformists and passionate dissenters; and this is more than simply a temperamental matter. It reflects the contradictory history they lived through, as well as the conflictive vantage-point from which they lived it. It also shapes the inner structure of their novels. It is not just a sociological fact, but a formative influence on their sensibility.

If history was visibly in the making in the Romantic period (which is therefore the great age of the historical novel), so was it in the early decades of the Industrial Revolution. It was not just a question of cotton mills, rural enclosures, hunger and class-struggle, but of the crystallising of a whole new sensibility, one appropriate to an England which was becoming for the first time a largely urban society. It was a matter of learning new disciplines and habits of feeling, new rhythms of time and organisations of space, new forms of repression, deference and self-fashioning. A whole new mode of human subjectivity was in the making, one which like the self-divided protagonists of Charlotte Brontë's fiction was both aspiring and frustrated, rootless and solitary yet resourceful and self-reliant.

The typical individual of the new social order, as Charlotte's heroines again reveal, was self-seeking and hard-headed, yet fragile and desperately exposed. It would be hard to think of a finer prototype of such individuals than three cultivated women who were compelled to work for their living in oppressive conditions. Largely unprotected, the sisters ventured out from the civilised enclave of their Yorkshire parsonage into a world in which, as governesses, they were forced to put their culture to work as a commodity. They were thus well-placed to chronicle the clashes between civility and brutality, culture and labour, self-expression and self-repression, which everywhere marked this new form of social existence.

What is most impressive is the courage with which they confronted these conflicts. A contemporary novelist like Dickens, one might claim, had not much choice in the matter: he had no experience to hand but the present. The Brontës, however, had been nourished on some rich legacies of myth and legend, folktale and fantasy. Yet they neither shrank defensively into this hermetic world, nor casually abandoned it for their contemporary moment. Instead, their fiction brings the two dimensions together in intricate ways, weaving Gothic and realism, fairytale and social documentary, into striking new configurations. What other English novel is at once as imaginatively audacious and tenaciously realistic as *Wuthering Heights*?

One result of this, at least in the case of Charlotte's novels, is a remarkable blending of different literary forms, which in this book, first published thirty years ago, I contrast unfavourably with the unity of Emily's great novel. Since it seems to me now that unity is no automatic virtue, and that much of the force of Charlotte's work springs from these incongruous conjunctures, this judgement strikes me today as highly suspect. So, too, does my consistent underplaying of the sisters' gender, a flagrant example of which is my callously nonchalant way with Lucy Snowe's sufferings as a vulnerable, isolated young woman in a foreign land. This is a pre-feminist study in what is nowadays for the most part a post-feminist world, and it bears the marks of it almost everywhere. Today, I would prefer to argue that gender is the place where all the other contradictions by which the sisters are besieged, and which this book tries to sketch, are most poignantly focused.

In the leftist Holy Trinity of class, race and gender, class in this study edges aside not only gender, but also race or ethnicity. Just as it is vitally significant that those great luminaries of English letters Swift, Goldsmith, Shaw, Wilde, Conrad, James, Pound, Yeats, Joyce, Beckett and T. S. Eliot were not English at all, so also is the fact that the Brontës, like so many other eminent contributors to the annals of English literature, were of Irish descent. Over the centuries, the Irish have not only had to pay rents and ship beef to the British; they have also had to write much of their finest literature for them. Certainly there would have been precious little English stage comedy without Irish immigrants, men who washed up on these shores with only their wit, a flair for language, and an outsider's eye for native absurdities to hawk.

The Brontës' mixed ethnic background is not ignored in this book, but neither is it granted the prominence I now believe it merits. Patrick, the sisters' eccentric, irascible father, was an Irishman from County Down, and even today 'Brontë country' for some of the Irish means the area of Ulster in which he was reared. The Brontës' wayward brother, also a Patrick, behaved throughout his brief, doomed existence like the English stereotype of the feckless Mick: idle, drunken, pugnacious, rebellious, extravagant, improvident, full of dishevelled fantasy.

Like many a stereotype, the standard view of the Irishman is interestingly ambivalent. If he is violent, dissolute and subversive, he is also passionate, warm-blooded and creative. It is a double-edgedness not all that remote from the character of Heathcliff in *Wuthering Heights*. The young Heathcliff—a 'dirty, ragged, black-haired child' who speaks 'a kind of gibberish'—is picked up starving off the streets of Liverpool by old Earnshaw, and the novel will later portray him as savage, lunatic, violent, rebellious and uncouth—all off-the-peg nineteenth-century English images of their Celtic colonials. Only a few months before Emily began the novel, her brother took a trip to Liverpool, where he could easily have observed some of the hundreds of semi-destitute Irish-speaking refugee children hanging around the docks. They were described in a national journal as dressed in rags with an animal growth of black hair—little Heathcliffs, in short. As Irish speakers, like almost all of the Irish poor at the time, they would have spoken what was indeed gibberish to English ears.[1]

Whether Heathcliff is actually Irish is no more demonstrable than whether he is actually a murderer. Fictional characters do not have a history: they are simply organisations of black marks on a page, and these words contain all that we can warrantably claim of them. There is no Hamlet before he strolls on stage, and his corpse lies eternally unburied. Even so, the profound ambiguity of Heathcliff is significant. Not only is he, like the sisters themselves, an insider/outsider: he is also an extraordinary amalgam of the creative and the destructive, high passion and vindictive cruelty, transcendent love and brutally self-interested machinations. *Wuthering*

---

1 I have written more fully on this subject in *Heathcliff and the Great Hunger* (London, 1995), and *The English Novel: An Introduction* (Oxford, 2004), ch. 6.

*Heights* makes no attempt to resolve these antinomies. Here as elsewhere, it simply presents us with mutually incompatible narratives or versions of reality, without signalling (as Charlotte would certainly have done) which ones to trust. We are deliberately prevented by the book's peculiar structure from assembling a coherent image of its male protagonist. The Grange has its truths, and so does the Heights; but the text resists our attempts to stitch the two neatly together.

Heathcliff, in old Earnshaw's words, could be a gift from God but is as dark as the devil, and this ambiguous angelic/demonic imagery pursues this enigmatic interloper throughout the narrative. The way he is treated by the Heights, so even the hostile Nelly Dean concedes, is enough to turn a saint into a fiend. In ancient society, the creature who was seen as both holy and cursed, innocent and polluted, lethal and life-bearing. was known as the *pharmakos* or scapegoat. The scapegoat is both poison and potential cure: it signifies a kind of dirt and defilement, but one which, if you have the courage to expose yourself to its ambiguous power, may prove strangely beneficent.

If the scapegoat is shut out of the city, the city will fail to see in its monstrosity an image of the violence and disfigurement which lie at its own foundation. The Grange in *Wuthering Heights* is a place of order and civility, but one which veils the hard labour and exploitation on which these virtues are based. In the Heights, by contrast, aggression and brutality are much more out in the open. If the ancient city has the courage to take the scapegoat in, as Athens finally embraces the cursed, blinded figure of Oedipus, a regenerative power is likely to flow from this deed. The Heights literally takes Heathcliff in, but spiritually shuts him out; and it is this which turns a potential blessing into a curse.[1] If this dark outsider does indeed have Irish roots, then there may be the ghost of an allegory here of the plagued, inside/outside relationship at the time between that nation and its colonial proprietors.

The *pharmakos* is a figure which seems to hover indeterminately between life and death. It is a deathly deformation of humanity, but as such reveals something of humanity's true condition. It has crossed an invisible threshold between life and death, and is already

1 For a fuller discussion of the tragic scapegoat, see my *Sweet Violence: The Idea of the Tragic* (Oxford, 2003), ch. 10.

living in some twilight realm beyond the daylight world of the living. In the language of Freud, this is the domain inhabited by those in the grip of the death drive; and Heathcliff, for Freudian theory, would be a prime example of such a figure. The implacable absolutism of his need for Catherine has a flavour of the absolutism of death. It is able to convert him into a living corpse, as when he stands motionless for hours outside his lover's window. It is by staying stubbornly constant to their ravaging desire for one another, in the teeth of conventional social *mores*, that Heathcliff and Catherine are carried on the current of that desire straight into the negativity of death. Only in this utterly impersonal sphere, at once sublimely transcendent and ruthlessly annihilating, will their 'relationship' (if so commonplace a term is appropriate) find fulfilment.

As both sacred and contaminated, the scapegoat is a 'high' and 'low' phenomenon at the same time. So, too, is the Romantic notion of vision, which is uncomfortably close to the rather less edifying idea of fantasy. It is one of the embarrassments of a post-Freudian age that we are aware of just how close the visionary imagination lies to the regressive make-believe of day dreaming. When the poet W. B. Yeats uses the word 'dream', he means idle fancy just about as often as he means prophetic insight. The faculty which is supposed to unlock the secrets of reality is also the place where you can flee from it. It is not surprising, then, that the Catherine–Heathcliff 'relationship' can be seen both as expressing a utopian vision at odds with the degraded present, and as a form of infantile regression.

There is another ambiguity of high and low, one more obvious in Charlotte's fiction than in Emily's. It is the process by which guilty desires are redeemed by being turned to more noble ends, a conversion technically known as 'sublimation'. I note in this book how almost all human relationships in the Brontës are essentially power struggles, and how (not least in the case of Charlotte's work) these conflicts commonly assume a sado-masochistic form. Deference, submission and domination, the pleasures of mastery and the delights of being ruled: these are all much in evidence in *Jane Eyre* and *Villette*, *Shirley* and *The Professor*. A grotesque, gratuitous violence also marks *Wuthering Heights*; but in that novel sadism is rather more in evidence than masochism, whereas Charlotte's fiction combines the two in remarkably intricate ways. There is an edgy, erotic perversity about human relationships in her writing, a constant splitting, fusing and inverting of gender roles which is far removed from anything we find in Jane Austen or George Eliot. Attraction and antagonism strike up curious alliances, as cross-currents of spite, humility, belligerence and self-laceration send their complex eddies throughout the narratives.

Once again, I try to show in the book how these are more than matters of simple temperament or individual psychology. On the contrary, they constitute what one might call the political unconscious of Charlotte's work. They represent the way in which the social and sexual contradictions she lived through are transmuted into a kind of psychic subtext of the novels. Revealed directly, that subtext would be too shocking for respectable literature; so its disreputable desires must be 'sublimated' by the novels' official storylines. A masochistic love of being mastered becomes a socially acceptable respect for authority, while the desire to dominate others becomes a mark of spiritual superiority.

Sado-masochism involves taking pleasure in the disciplining or chastising of the self; and this, one might claim, is Charlotte's version of the death drive which we have noted at work in her sister's great novel. The key difference is that death, in Charlotte's case, is pressed into the service of life. I mean by this that the 'little death' of self-abasement and humiliation, in the case of a Jane Eyre or Lucy Snowe, is a prelude to worldly success. It is Jane's nun-like meekness which will help her to become Mrs Rochester. The 'death' of dutiful submission turns out in Charlotte's work to have a definite exchange-value in terms of status, property and self-fulfilment. One must sacrifice the self up to a point, not least because it is perversely pleasurable to do so; but at the same time, in Jane Eyre's words, one must keep in good health and not die.

This is not true of Emily's novel, whose hero and heroine fail to keep in good health and die. *Wuthering Heights* is tragic not least because there is no exchange-value at stake here, no calculable return on the reckless expenditure of its protagonists. In fact, they may not rest quiet even in death. *Wuthering Heights* is an otherworldly novel not because it trades in mythology and spiritual symbolism, but because it has little interest in material advancement or individual progress, those mighty fetishes of its age. In this sense, it is otherworldly in all the most disturbing, disruptive ways. At its core lies something alien and recalcitrant, some need or passion which resists being fully articulated, and which for both good and ill plays havoc with the stability of the social order. It also plays havoc with the stability of the classical realist text, garbling its chronology, embedding one narrative within another like Chinese boxes, and refusing the reader a reassuring voice-over.

The Brontë sisters are one of those idiosyncratic English phenomena which might well give one the impression of having sprung from nowhere. They were certainly displaced, out-of-joint, contradictory figures; but I try to show in this study how, paradoxically, it is precisely in that sense of being adrift and disinherited that they are most typical of a whole historical epoch.

T. E.
2004

# Introduction to the Second Edition

This book was first published in 1975, on the very threshold of a major resurgence of Marxist criticism in Britain. Since the radical political events of the late 1960s, Marxist criticism had been much in the air; but when *Myths of Power* first appeared, the chief theoretical formulations of this critical current were still to emerge. My own work of Marxist literary theory, *Criticism and Ideology*, appeared one year later in 1976; the following year witnessed the publication of Raymond Williams' important *Marxism and Literature*, and 1978 saw the English translation of Pierre Macherey's influential *A Theory of Literary Production*. From 1976 onwards, a series of annual conferences on Marxist literary and cultural theory were held at the University of Essex, bringing physically together for the first time a large number of young radical critics whose work and political allegiances had been shaped in the aftermath of Paris 1968.[1] But *Myths of Power* was a straw in this impending political gale; and like all premature or prefigurative phenomena, it was unable to reap the benefits of the whirlwind it presaged.

Perhaps something of the climate of those years can be suggested by a minor anecdote. I remember a friend of mine, himself a distinguished Marxist critic, asking me somewhat apprehensively whether I actually intended to use the term 'Marxist' in the subtitle of the book, and on being told that I did, expressing a kind of awed admiration for what seemed to him – but not particularly to me – a boldly heterodox, even rashly provocative gesture. In 1975, in other words, it was still not considered entirely 'safe' actually to *declare* oneself as a Marxist, even if

---

1 A representative selection of papers from these pioneering conferences is now available as *Literature, Politics & Theory*, ed. F. Barker, P. Hulme, M. Iverson and D. Loxley (Methuen, 1986).

one's work implicitly bore that particular stamp. Perhaps my friend's caution was justified, judging by some of the reviews which the book received. The former Communist Philip Toynbee, reviewing the book in the *Observer* newspaper, spent almost all of the available space discussing the *Dedication*. One had heard of reviewers who gave up after the first couple of chapters, or even after the Introduction, but to get no further than the Dedication suggested a feebleness of application on Toynbee's part which in a schoolchild would probably mean weekly visits to an educational therapist. Toynbee largely confined his review to a few jeers at the names of my children, in the characteristically generous, sensitive style of the liberal humanist; but at least he did not take the work to be some kind of sinister practical joke, which was how it was received by one or two of the Brontë 'trade journals'. These publications, which specialise in discussions of such matters as the size of Charlotte's hands (as deducible from a recently discovered pair of gloves), greeted the book with befuddled incredulity, as a theological journal might greet a study arguing that John the Baptist was a Trotskyite. By the end of the 1970s, Marxist criticism was perhaps no dearer to the hearts of reviewers than it was to the shortwinded Toynbee; but the ideological climate had nevertheless decisively changed. It was now painfully obvious, as it was perhaps not in 1975, that this brash new form of materialist analysis was not simply going to go away if one did not stare too hard at it; and by the early 1980s it had to be acknowledged, in the words of a director of a major British publishing house, that for the first time since the 1930s all the most exciting criticism was coming from the political left.

If *Myths of Power* was in that sense prefigurative, it was also fated, as I have suggested, to miss out on some of the benefits of the intellectual currents it anticipated. One way in which that is obvious to me now is in the work's somewhat uneasy conjuncture of a relatively sophisticated Marxist *theory* with a fairly conventional critical *practice*. The discussions of particular novels, Charlotte's in particular, still adhere too much to the orthodox paradigm of 'practical criticism', the familiar, blow-by-blow 'close reading' of the celebrated 'words on the page'. Marxist criticism must of course *read* the texts it examines, and read them closely; but we have become more alert since the mid 1970s to the problematic question of what it means to read, and the critical readings offered here are to my mind too little transformed in method by the literary theory which surrounds them. At this probationary point, in other words, a fully adequate interaction of radical theory and transformative reading practice has yet to be achieved; 'theory' and 'practice' lie too much as separated idioms within the same pages, and only the account of *Wuthering Heights* seems to me now to press some way beyond this disjuncture. The chapter on the structure of Charlotte's fiction provides some essential counterballast to this critical conventionalism, addressing as it does some deeper interrelations of literary form and social ideology; and it appears to me now that it is here, on the whole, that the book's strengths lie, rather than in its more local analyses of this or that incident or character in the fiction.

The kind of Marxist literary theory informing the book is much endebted to the work of Lucien Goldmann, with its notion of 'categorial structures' as key mediations between literary form, textual ideology and social relations. These connections still seem to me the most vital for any Marxist criticism; but I would be considerably more critical today of Goldmann's excessively 'homologous' model, which always seems to presume that the various 'levels' of analysis involved – historical forces, ideologies or 'world visions', the inner structure of the literary text itself – will reproduce one another without undue conflict or contradiction. Goldmann's so-called 'genetic structuralism' suffers in this sense from the egregious defects of structuralism in general, with its covertly organicist impulse towards totalised unities; and *Myths of Power* is frequently guilty of such 'over-totalisation'. It fails on the whole to practise the kind of critical method I was to lay out one year later in *Criticism and Ideology*, where the literary text itself is grasped less as 'expressive' of an underlying ideology or historical situation, than as a 'production' or transformation of these elements into a quite new configuration. The study, that is to say, remains too 'expressivist' in its fundamental critical viewpoint, too easily convinced that the structure of the literary text can be viewed simply as a 'transposition' of a wider, underlying organisation of forces. The danger of such a method is an idealism every bit as disabling as in orthodox liberal–humanist criticism: an unwitting suppression of the materiality of the text itself, with its specific productive strategies and devices, its transfigurative semiotic codes.

Even so, I must confess to being a little impressed by how well on the whole this now somewhat discredited 'Marxist–structuralist' method stands up in an approach to the Brontës. It has become clear since 1975 that structuralism and Marxism, as general 'world views', are radically incompatible, and 'high' structuralism has long since passed out of vogue. But this is not to say that certain structuralist concepts cannot be salvaged from the philosophical rubble and put to use; and indeed I would want now to be rather more pluralistic about the question of Marxist critical method than I probably was in writing this book. Where Marxism diverges from pluralism seems to me over the question of its political goals: there can be no ultimate compromise between support for a ruling social order and a commitment to those forces which seek to undermine it, and the notion of a 'middle ground' between these two options strikes me as an ideological illusion. But the *promotion* of those goals can involve a whole range of theoretical and political strategies, the validity of which is to be assessed not absolutely or immanently, but in the light of what they may achieve. It is this which distinguishes a necessary methodological pluralism from a simple liberalism or eclecticism. The 'structuralist' components of this book seem to me to serve their purpose well enough, even if structuralism as a whole ideology is finally inimical to historical materialist thought. I remember one or two Marxist colleagues in the later 1970s reacting rather sharply to what they took to be the illicit blending of approaches in this study: some Goldmann here, a little Macherey there, a touch of Lukács or Althusser elsewhere. But this now seems to me to reveal more about the fetishism of method which characterised some of the work of that period, including my own, rather than to pinpoint an essential flaw or confusion in the book itself.

What classical structuralism finally yielded ground to was what we now know as 'post-structuralism', which was at the time of original publication well under way in Europe but still only a rumour in Britain. A typical post-structuralist critique of *Myths of Power* would doubtless claim that it works too centrally with various kinds of binary oppositions it fails to deconstruct: bourgeois rationalism and Romantic conservatism, masculine and feminine, realism and imaginative fantasy, rebellion and conformity. There is, no doubt, something in this claim; but I was particularly concerned in Chapter 5 to demonstrate how these polarities do indeed constantly undo and invert themselves in the course of Charlotte's fiction, and to argue moreover for the ideological necessity of such displacements and reversals. To that extent, the study might be taken to illustrate how a certain deconstruction need not simply abandon all historical or political responsibility, euphorically dissolving complex contradiction into sheer indeterminability or some myth of pure difference. What post-structuralist accounts of the Brontës have appeared in the wake of this book strike me as running precisely those risks.[1] On the other hand, post-structuralist criticism has alerted us to certain effects of literary form which this book too little reckons into account. The chapter on *Wuthering Heights* seeks to locate the widely agreed strengths of that text in its *unifying* power: its capacity to weld together conflicts into a coherent 'vision' which remains formally unfissured by the turbulent materials it encompasses. Charlotte's fiction, by contrast, is (so I argue) considerably more diffuse, uneven and formally incoherent; and the comparison is intended as a negative judgement on her work. Whatever particular insights this case may permit, its whole theoretical basis now strikes me as radically mistaken. It is, in effect, the position of a Georg Lukács, who celebrates those forms which serenely transcend and encompass the contradictions of their content. Such an attitude led Lukács to a dogmatic, politically catastrophic denunciation of the deliberately mixed, conflictive, open-ended theatrical forms of a Bertolt Brecht.[2] There is a sense in which, in this study, Emily is made to play Lukács to Charlotte's Brecht. What the book has to say about the formal slippages and discrepancies of Charlotte's novels still seems to me true; the negative value-judgement which such techniques incur is much more dubious. It is notable, for instance, that whereas 'myth', when used of *Wuthering Heights*, is on the whole a positive term, no such indulgence is typically extended to Charlotte's uses of it in such novels as *Shirley*. Instead, it is too quickly equated with a kind of 'unreal' fantasy, and thus largely written off. The book is conscious of a 'problem of how to write' in the Brontës; but rather than examining the ideological determinants of that dilemma, it turns prematurely to conventional value-judgement, underscoring 'realist' effects in Charlotte and suspiciously interrogating those aspects of her writing which cannot be accommodated to this traditional model.

Throughout the study, in other words, there is a strongly realist aesthetics implicitly at work, which in part determines the way

1 See, for example, J. Hillis Miller's discussion of *Wuthering Heights* in his *Fiction and Repetition* (Basil Blackwell, 1982), which in a characteristic gesture of American deconstruction grandly surveys a range of critical approaches to the novel only to conclude that they are all without exception rendered partial or illicit by the text's indeterminability. The deconstructionist is thus able to worst every other critic at a stroke without adopting anything like a 'position' of his or her own. The implicit politics of this gesture repay some study.
2 For a record of the 1930s debate between the two critics, see E. Bloch *et al*, *Aesthetics and Politics* (New Left Books, 1977).

Charlotte's novels are actually read. But what if this were not the most appropriate frame for such a reading? What if the remarkable plurality and discrepancy of *genres* in her work were itself one of its most significant features, a radical *challenge* to orthodox realism rather than a thoughtless deviation from it? Much has been written since 1975, and something had been written even before then, of the woman writer's necessary resistance to those seamless, organic, homogenous literary forms which have been the traditional prerogative of men; and in that light it would have been possible to offer a more positive interpretation of Charlotte's multiple fictions as part of a tradition of feminine deconstruction. *Myths of Power*, however, almost entirely excludes such feminist considerations, and seems only sporadically conscious of the fact that its chosen authors are women. There are two reasons for this exclusion, one rather more reputable than the other. The more reputable reason is that just as this book appeared on the very brink of a major outgrowth of Marxist criticism in the later 1970s, so it predated most of the influential studies in feminist criticism which were a few years later to achieve classic status. Ellen Moers's *Literary Women* was published in 1976, Elaine Showalter's *A Literature of their Own* appeared one year later, and Sandra Gilbert and Susan Gubar's *The Madwoman in the Attic*, whose very title evokes Charlotte's Bertha Rochester, came out in 1979. Feminist criticism in the USA was already strongly developed in the early 1970s, but perhaps rather less strongly so in Britain. Even so, feminist criticism in this country was much in the air; and there was thus no good reason to ignore it. The more disreputable motive for the book's exclusion of feminist preoccupations then, is also a banally familiar one: the infamous 'gender blindness' of traditional Marxist theory. Indeed there are points in *Myths of Power* where this stubborn myopia achieves well-nigh farcical proportions. In one of the very few passages in the study even to consider what I still rather quaintly term the 'woman question', I write of the Brontë sisters as '*isolated* educated women, socially and geographically remote from a world with which they nonetheless maintained close intellectual touch, and so driven back on themselves in solitary emotional hungering'. The very next sentence comments '. . . that loneliness becomes type and image of the isolation of all *men* in an individualist society' (my italics). For men, as they say, read women. Some remarks on *Villette*, even more absurdly, claim that 'there is little in (the novel) . . . to motivate Lucy's emotional torment'. Nothing indeed, except for the fact that she is a lonely, frustrated, exploited woman in a predatory male society.

The theoretical model with which this book works is not in itself, I think, class-reductionist. On the contrary, true to its Althusserian background, it emphasises the 'overdetermination' of the Brontës's fiction, the multiple, interacting constituents of its making. In practice, however, many of these non-class determinants, and gender above all, are given notably short shrift. As the Marxist–feminist collective of London wrote: '(Eagleton's) treatment of Jane Eyre herself as an asexual representative of the upwardly-mobile bourgeoisie leads to a reductionist reading of the text. It neglects gender as a determinant, by subsuming gender under class. The meritocratic vision of 'individual self-reliance', as Eagleton puts it, *cannot* be enacted by a woman character in the same way as it can be by a male'.[1] I would want to argue now that the question of gender, far from figuring in the Brontës as one among many social determinants, is nothing less than the *dominant medium* in which, in much of their writing at least, other social conflicts are actually lived out; and it has its own high degree of autonomy of those other conflicts too. To fail to recognise this is not only to produce a seriously limited analysis, but to err in *tone*. If much of the critical treatment of Jane Eyre, Lucy Snowe and Shirley is markedly unsympathetic, even at time briskly impatient, this may not only be on account of a characteristic male anxiety (and hence defensiveness) when confronted with images of the emotionally hungering woman; it is also because I am attending less to the woman than to the *petty bourgeoise*, displacing the focus from gender to class, and thus directing towards the former negative judgements and responses which might have a certain justification in the case of the latter.

This is not to argue, on the other hand, that the class status of the Brontës's protagonists should be simply suppressed – that they can be exculpated because of their gender, in some falsely chivalric gesture. On the contrary, there are indeed negative, even offensive aspects of these characters which spring more or less directly from their class positions; the Charlotte Brontë who has been properly redeemed and valorised by feminist criticism is also the woman who deeply feared workers' revolution in Britain and indulged in the crudest travesty of working-class characters. What feminist criticism of the Brontës has appeared since the first publication of this book has not, on the whole, addressed

---

1 'Women's Writing: *Jane Eyre, Shirley, Villette, Aurora Leigh*', in F. Barker *et al* (eds.), *1848: The Sociology of Literature* (University of Essex, 1978) p. 191.

itself to these issues.[1] Indeed it has been in general as unhistorical and class-blind as traditional Marxist criticism has been obstinately oblivious of gender. Feminist criticism may have good reasons for this omission, as Marxist criticism does not: its understandable fear of appropriation by male radicals has led it perhaps to give somewhat less than full attention to those aspects of women's oppression about which Marxism has something relevant to say. But it cannot be ignored either that the brunt of contemporary feminist criticism has emerged from the society in the world today most deeply hostile to socialism, and these political conditions may well have left their mark. Since the later 1970s, much Marxist criticism, however blunderingly, externally or even patronisingly, has sought to engage with questions of women's oppression, and in this way to make what reparation it can for past omissions. The same, to date at least, cannot in general be said of feminist criticism's relation to Marxism.

Feminist criticism in our time has struck up a kind of logical alliance with psychoanalytical theory; and the latter is another palpable silence in this book. The chapter on *Wuthering Heights*, though not, I think, a 'Romantic' reading of the text, is nevertheless too ready to take on board such essentially Romantic concepts as 'the imagination', 'authenticity' and 'liberation', without submitting these notions to Freud's sceptical, rigorously materialist reading. Despite its own materialist bias, there is an aura of idealism about that whole account, which a judicious dose of Freudianism might well have tempered.[2] The disruptive force of the unconscious is evident enough in the libidinal exchanges of that text; but its traces can also be found in the curious nature of the *writing*, another matter to which I here give insufficient consideration. The implicit epistemology of this book is in many ways more idealist than materialist: high marks are awarded to works which achieve some 'balance' of subjective and objective, and censorious comments are provoked by texts which are in some sense disjunctive, subjectively 'excessive' or non-totalised. *Wuthering Heights* is accordingly congratulated on its high degree of formal unity; but this simply overlooks the fact that, with its

1 See, for example, the chapter on the Brontës in S. Gilbert and S. Gubar, *The Madwoman in the Attic* (New Haven, 1979), and the chapter on *Villette* in Mary Jacobus, *Reading Woman* (Ithaca, New York, 1986). A notable exception is Judith Lowder Newton's account of *Villette* in her *Women, Power and Subversion* (University of Georgia, 1981).
2 For a valuable Marxist–Freudian interpretation of *Wuthering Heights*, see James Kavanagh, *Emily Brontë* (Basil Blackwell, 1985).

'Chinese boxes' effect of narratives-within-narratives, its constant regression of perspectives and instabilities of viewpoint, it is a strangely 'decentred' fiction which subverts the dominance of the conventional authorial 'voice' as markedly as aspects of its subject-matter threaten to undermine the received forms of bourgeois society. In concentrating on the bizarre features of the world of the Heights, I miss the most bizarre phenomenon of all: the elusive, enigmatic text of *Wuthering Heights* itself.

There are other faults or exclusions in this study which I would now want to repair. The Brontë sisters have entered the canon of English literature, but their background was not English at all; they were Irish by descent, as Heathcliff may well be too.[1] Women and the Irish were sometimes coupled together in the Victorian imagination as equally 'childlike' outsiders, affectionate but irrational; and it would have been interesting to explore this issue in the book. I look at the myths of the Brontës, but not enough at the myth of the Brontës: the construction and reconstruction of the sisters in critical history, for varying ideological purposes. The Brontës, like Shakespeare, are a literary industry as well as a collection of literary texts, and it would have been worth asking why this should be so and how it came about. Finally, I would now want to qualify what seems to me rather too rigid a contrast between the 'politics' of Emily's text, and those of Charlotte's. In the end, Charlotte emerges here as a compromiser and canny strategist, in contrast with the unflinching absolutism I discern in *Wuthering Heights*. Such a judgement not only passes over the powerfully 'incorporative' aspects of the latter work, but underplays the radicalism of the former. In *social* terms, Charlotte's novels indeed negotiate adroitly for an acceptable settlement; but this decorous resolution is constantly jeopardised by a *sexual* demand – an angry, wounded, implacable desire for full personal acceptance and recognition – which breaks beyond the boundaries of any social or narrative closure. The book's strategy tends to generate too severe an opposition between the two sisters in this respect; and I leave it to the reader to deconstruct that polarity as he or she might wish.

T.E.
1987

1 See Winifred Gerin, *Emily Brontë* (O.U.P., 1971) pp. 225–226.

# Introduction

If it is no longer fashionable to see the Brontës simply as a marooned, metaphysical trio, sublimely detached from their historical milieu, it is equally true that 'historical' readings of their fiction still evoke a degree of suspicion. Can the measure of that passionate intensity truly be taken by the blundering techniques of some literary sociology? Do we not find in, say, that sense of an ultimate bedrock of being which haunts Catherine Earnshaw in *Wuthering Heights*, a supreme instance of great art's resistance to any merely sociological rendering?

Of course, so the standard argument runs, 'sociology' has its place. '*Wuthering Heights*', remarks Mrs Q. D. Leavis, 'is remarkably similar to *Great Expectations*. The latter too is a work of art which also contains a sociological novel on the surface.'[1] There are works of literature which seem sociological in bias, and when these come our way we call in the sociological critic to attend to them – to supplement, with his own specialist and 'surface' reading, those more inward accounts which a critic proper (one whose concern is with the centrally human rather than the contingently social) may provide. The strategy of orthodox liberal criticism is no longer to deny the validity of a 'social' interpretation of literary texts; that particular Cold War is fading with its political counterpart, and the conjunction doesn't seem fortuitous. We are all Marxists now, even those of us who are still liberals. 'In this book', announces Donald Davie in the foreword to his *Thomas Hardy and British Poetry*, 'I have taken it for granted that works of literary art are conditioned by economic and political forces active in the society from which those works spring and to which they are directed. . . .'[2] 'Criticism', remarked Graham Hough a few years earlier, 'should be able to give some intelligible account of the relation of literature to the social order. There is a methodology for this, and so far as I know there is only one. To think on this subject at all requires some application of Marxism. . . .'[3] Faced with such generosity after so many years in the cold, it seems churlish of Marxist criticism to hesitate in its glad response – churlish, certainly, to linger paranoically over the casualness of Davie's 'I have taken it for granted' or the cautiousness of Hough's 'some application'. And one's embarrassment is compounded by the knowledge that the only authentic response to such good-natured accommodation is bound to appear indecently arrogant. Since, however, both Davie and Hough imply a strictly subsidiary role for Marxist criticism, that response needs to be formulated. The historical critic does not approach a literary text as the ornithologist might approach *The Ancient Mariner*, or the horticulturalist *The Garden*. His founding assumption – it has surely been said often enough – is that all novels are political novels, all drama historical drama, all poems social poems. If Marxist criticism can illuminate Disraeli but not Daniel, *The Deserted Village* but not the *Ode to Evening*, then it is indeed some mere 'sociology of literature' and deserves to be treated as such. Marxist criticism must refuse to occupy its modest niche within that formidable array of critical methods – mythological, psychoanalytic, theological, stylistic – which reflects the tolerant pluralism of a liberal democracy. It cannot endorse that division of critical labour – cannot, by definition, view itself merely as a one-sided contribution to the great Hegelian totality of truth. By its nature, it must claim to shift the terrain of that debate, rather than to rest content as one component within it. It is by that claim, exacting as it is, that a Marxist criticism stands or falls.

Merely to declare all literature social is so extreme an exercise in formalism that as it stands it does no more than empty both terms of content. What the declaration signifies, however, seems to me a good deal less empty. It suggests that the 'social' or 'historical' are never merely extra terms, to be blandly equated with others; they have, actually and methodologically, a radical priority of status. The 'social' in literature is never merely a surface layer, a question of coal-mines and speech-mannerisms; it is the matrix within which all other terms are fleshed and shaped. Q. D. Leavis's metaphor of the sociological novel draped across the surface of *Wuthering Heights* graphically expresses the alienation of a society whose own character *as* society has become casually extraneous to it.

Yet this does little to broach the question of how literature and society are actually related. What relationship holds between the imaginative fiction of the Brontës and the society of their time? We may first dispel in purely empirical fashion the myth of the three weird sisters deposited on the Yorkshire moors from some metaphysical outer space. The Brontës' home, Haworth, was close to the centre of the West Riding woollen area; and their lifetime there coincided with some of the fiercest class-struggles in English society. The years of their childhood were years of ruination for thousands of hand-workers dispersed in hill-cottages around the region – men and women who drifted, destitute, to the villages and towns. They lived, in short, through an aspect of the events which Karl Marx described in *Capital* as the most horrible tragedy of English history.[4] Their childhood witnessed machine-breaking; their adolescence Reform agitation and riots against the New Poor Law; their adulthood saw the Plug strikes and Chartism, struggles against the Corn Laws and for the Ten Hours Bill. 'During the 1830s and '40s', Eric Hobsbawm has reminded us, '[the West Riding] was perhaps the firmest stronghold of violent Radicalism and Chartism in the North.'[5] His opinion was shared by Sir Charles Napier, Governor of the Northern Division head-quarters at Halifax, who wrote in 1841 that 'Every element of a ferocious civil war is boiling in the district'.[6] Haworth itself, far from forming some idyllic oasis of pre-industrial peace, had several worsted mills and a more than century-old industry; and despite Mrs Gaskell's assertion that its population was not on the whole poor,[7] the sisters would certainly have seen a good deal of destitution on their own doorstep.

Salutary though a reminder of the Brontës' historical situation may be, it leaves in suspension the problem of critical method – of how the fiction is to be rooted in, without being reduced to, specific social conditions. It seems clear that the connection we are pursuing here cannot consist in the mere relating of empirical literary facts to empirical social facts – cannot, that is to say, be simply a crude one-to-one correlation of literary and social detail, in the manner of some vulgar literary sociology. What must

be in question here is some concept of *structure*. I am concerned in
this study to identify in the Brontës' fiction a recurrent 'categorial
structure' of roles, values and relations, and, since this informing
structure seems to me distinctly ideological, to claim this as a
primary mediation between the novels and society, a crucial nexus
between fiction and history. I take the phrase 'categorial structure'
from the Marxist critic Lucien Goldmann, who uses it to designate
those shared categories which inform apparently heterogeneous
works, and shape the consciousness of the particular social group
or class which produces them. Since my admiration for Goldmann's
work is laced with strong reservations, my use of the concept in
this book will be deliberately free, even though, like Goldmann,
I shall employ it as an essential mediation between literary text,
social consciousness and historical forces. By 'categorial structure',
then, I seek to identify the inner ideological structure of a work,
and to expose its relations both to what we call literary 'form' and
to an actual history.[8]

   That ideological structure arises from the real history of the
West Riding in the first half of the nineteenth century; and it is,
I believe, imaginatively grasped and transposed in the production
of the Brontës' fiction. We find embedded in Charlotte's work, for
example, a constant struggle between two ambiguous, internally
divided sets of values. On the one hand are ranged the values of
rationality, coolness, shrewd self-seeking, energetic individualism,
radical protest and rebellion; on the other hand lie the habits of
piety, submission, culture, tradition, conservatism. I call these
patterns of value 'ambiguous' because the elements of one may
be displaced or 'inverted' into the other; and this, indeed, is precisely the point. For it is possible to decipher in the conflicts and
compromises between them a fictionally transformed version of the
tensions and alliances between the two social classes which dominated the Brontës' world: the industrial bourgeoisie, and the landed
gentry or aristocracy. I read Charlotte's novels as 'myths' which
work towards a balance or fusion of blunt bourgeois rationality
and flamboyant Romanticism, brash initiative and genteel cultivation, passionate rebellion and cautious conformity; and those
interchanges embody a complex structure of convergence and antagonism between the landed and industrial sectors of the contemporary ruling class.

The actual relations between landed and industrial classes in the Brontës' time were notably fluid and complex.[9] It seems clear that, despite real clashes of political and economic interests, the distance between the classes was never unbridgeable. Even though the landed gentry tended not to marry into manufacturing families unless those families had achieved at least second-generation respectability, there was a considerable fusion of economic interests, as manufacturers bought up estates and landowners became deeply involved in industrial projects. John Marshall, a Leeds flax-spinner, bought land extensively in Cumberland, Lancashire and the North Riding and set up his four sons as squires; William Denison, a highly respected West Riding manufacturer, became a major landowner in Nottinghamshire and Lincolnshire; the Wakefield Milnes family, owners of the second largest firm in the woollen industry, virtually withdrew their capital from trade to land at a crucial stage of the first period of industrialisation. On the other hand there were men like Walter Spencer-Stanhope, son of a woollen merchant and owner of 11,000 acres in Yorkshire, who became keenly engaged in West Riding industry. Landowners became promoters of turnpikes, canals, ports and banks, while the children of wealthy merchants who had bought land in the eighteenth century received such a fine education that they emerged as country gentlemen more genteel than the gentry themselves. Traditional landed society easily assimilated these rich merchant families; county families moved at ease with industrial magnates, and in the early decades of the nineteenth century a new osmosis between gentry and manufacturers took place, on the basis of a growing eighteenth-century alliance of interests. The landed gentry thus provided a kind of safety-valve for some of the pressure of new industrial wealth. The landed aristocracy, through its national and metropolitan political role, was inescapably confronted with the problems of the new society generated by coal, steam and iron; and since it was on the whole prepared to come to terms with these realities, the lower gentry – more parochial and conservative than the aristocracy, but politically dependent on them – had perforce to follow suit. The landed aristocracy increased in material strength and social standing throughout the nineteenth century, but at the same time the relative importance of agriculture and the wealth of the landed class in relation to other classes suffered a sharp decline.

On the one hand, then, traditional aristocrats became industrial entrepreneurs on a considerable scale; on the other hand, the industrial bourgeoisie looked to traditional landed authority to stabilise property in the turbulent conditions created by the presence of a militant working class. The West Riding, with its combination of large estates and industrial centres, was of particular significance here: its population grew by 73 per cent between 1801 and 1831,[10] but despite its industrial expansion it retained enormous estates. As the largest electoral constituency in the country, it had to share power and territory with growing commercial and industrial interests; and indeed, if there had been a single manufacturing interest it might well have commanded a political majority. Earl Fitzwilliam, owner of a large South Yorkshire colliery, ironworks, and property in Sheffield, was the figurehead for a Whig party organisation in which the leading liberals of Leeds, Bradford and Sheffield had at least half a share in management; so that while the Whig aristocrats could still dominate Whig political interests in the West Riding, they could do so only on the terms of an alliance with the bourgeoisie. The patterns of political power seem exceptionally complex, and certainly not directly reducible to the expression of economic interests: traditional family loyalties sometimes counted for more than such interests when the mineowners, railway directors and town-planners among the West Riding gentry turned to politics. Earl Fitzwilliam, ideologically a free-trader, objected to the methods of the anti-Corn Law League and was a major opponent; but it seems plausible that those members of the gentry who had become industrialists were less apprehensive of bourgeois threats to the agrarian interest than were Southern corn-growing squires who were solely dependent on agriculture. (The two greatest Tory mineowners in England, the Marquis of Londonderry and the Earl of Lonsdale, were divided over the issue of repealing the Corn Laws.)

At the level of parliamentary politics, of course, the landowners retained control in the West Riding, all of whose MPs between 1830 and 1885, with the exception of Cobden and the Halifax carpet manufacturer Crossley, emerged from that class. Cobden was returned to Parliament in 1847, on the initiative of Leeds free-traders who considered that the Whigs had failed to give their interests the weight they warranted; and his election caused deep indignation among many Whigs and all Tories, affronted as they were by the fact that he was a manufacturer and a non-Yorkshireman at that. When Cobden retired as M.P. in 1857, however, the traditional Whig position recovered with the election of an aristocrat. The pattern, then, was one of growing urban power, to which the Whig gentry ('the aristocratic representatives of the bourgeoisie', as Marx termed them) needed to adapt. Beneath the sporadic political confrontations between the two classes lay a steady convergence of interests, inherited from centuries of rapprochement between the industrial bourgeoisie and a capitalist landowning class with, as Frederick Engels remarked, 'habits and tendencies far more bourgeois than feudal'.[11]

How then are the Brontës to be situated within this social landscape? How does authorial biography intersect with broader social and ideological structures? There seems no doubt that contemporary criticism is confronted, among other methodological difficulties, with a problem of the *author*. Indeed it is here, ironically, that 'New Criticism' and vulgar Marxism link hands in a common dilemma. The former, unable to grasp anything but a disreputably Cartesian notion of intentionality, alienates the author from his product and in doing so severs one particular nerve between text and history. The latter, by reducing the author to some anonymous 'class-representative', the passive, replaceable bearer of historical forces, fails to understand the dialectics whereby an individual life actively transforms the historical structures which determine it into a unique artistic product. 'Valéry', Jean-Paul Sartre has remarked, 'is a petty-bourgeois intellectual, no doubt about it. But not every petty-bourgeois intellectual is Valéry.'[12]

Not every nineteenth-century petty-bourgeois intellectual was a Brontë. The Brontës lived through an era of disruptive social change, and lived that disruption at a peculiarly vulnerable point. For from being sublimely secluded from their history, that history entered, shaped and violated the inmost recesses of their personal lives. Indeed, so finely meshed were the strands which bound their history and biography into unity that one needs, to interpret their situation, to draw on a concept which Louis Althusser has borrowed from Freud – that of 'overdetermination'.[13] By 'overdetermination', Althusser seeks to describe the way in which major contradictions in society never emerge in 'pure' form; on the contrary, they act by condensing into complex unity an accumulated host of subsidiary conflicts, each of which conversely determines the general contradiction. The Brontës' situation is, I believe, overdetermined in precisely this sense. The major historical conflict which this book selects as its focus – that between landed and industrial capital – is sharpened and complicated for the Brontës by a host of subsidiary factors. Their situation is unique, certainly – but unique in its classical condensing of an unusually wide range of historical tensions. They happened to live in a region which revealed the friction between land and industry in peculiarly stark form – starker, certainly, than in a purely agrarian or industrial area. The same part of the country, as we have seen, witnessed working-class struggle at an extraordinary pitch of militancy, and in that sense too highlighted certain 'typical' historical trends. These pervasive social conflicts were then peculiarly intensified by the sisters' personal situation. They were, to begin with, placed at a painfully ambiguous point in the social structure, as the daughters of a clergyman with the inferior status of 'perpetual curate' who had thrust his way up from poverty; they strove as a family to maintain reasonably 'genteel' standards in a traditionally rough-and-ready environment. They were, moreover, socially insecure *women* – members of a cruelly oppressed gróup whose victimised condition reflected a more widespread exploitation. And they were *educated* women, trapped in an almost intolerable deadlock between culture and economics – between imaginative aspiration and the cold truth of a society which could use them merely as 'higher' servants. They were *isolated* educated women, socially and geographically remote from a world with which they nonetheless maintained close intellectual touch, and so driven back on themselves in solitary emotional hungering. At certain points in their fiction, indeed, that loneliness becomes type and image of the isolation of all men in an individualist society. And as if all this were not enough, they were forced to endure in their childhood an especially brutal form of ideological oppression – Calvinism.

In the unique imaginative formation of the Brontës, then, social, sexual, cultural, religious and geographical issues fuse into an over-determined unity. It is for this reason that we can trace in their very 'eccentricity' the contours of a common condition, detect in their highly specific life-style the unfolding of a general grammar. In a society where banishment from a centre seemed a general experience, the Brontës' 'eccentric' situation begins to seem curiously typical.

We need, however, to be rather more precise about their ambiguous social standing. Their father, Patrick Brontë, was the son of a poor Irish peasant family who had fought their way from cabin to cottage to tenant-farm; he himself was by turns blacksmith, linen-weaver and schoolmaster, and finally blazed a trail to Cambridge and Anglican orders. Marx's general characterisation of the petty bourgeoisie – 'contradiction incarnate' – seems in his case peculiarly apt. His bigoted poem *Vision of Hell*, for instance, is socially radical, dooming to torment the clergy, bailiffs and land-lords who exploit the poor;[14] yet as Tom Winnifrith points out,[15] his adoption of the name 'Brontë', boasts of aristocratic Cambridge friendships and cryptic hints of noble ancestry show how calculatedly he cut his roots, to become a fiercely anti-Luddite reactionary. His Low Church Evangelicalism reproduced his social ambivalence in religious terms, equally hostile as it was to prole-tarian Dissent and upper-class formalism. At Haworth too, there was the influence of the rigidly conformist Aunt Branwell, uneasy in the dour conditions of Yorkshire, fastidiously regretting the superior Cornish stock from which she came. A crisis of social identity, then, was endemic in this Tory, socially respectable but none too affluent family; Patrick Brontë could finance a fitting education for his daughters at Cowan Bridge school, but mainly because of its special provisions for the children of clerics.

The sisters' entry into Cowan Bridge school and then Roe Head marks the moment of their traumatic break from the imaginative freedom of the parsonage to an inflexibly disciplined, harshly restrictive regime. That crucial transition from sheltered settlement to crippling social pressure haunts their novels as a kind of primordial Fall, a spiritual rupture impossible to erase from memory. From here on, the sisters move into an exhausting confrontation with practical necessity which only Charlotte was to survive.

Charlotte speaks of school-life as 'wretched bondage'; Emily, of whom Charlotte wrote that 'Liberty was the breath of [her] nostrils', found the deadening routine of Roe Head unendurable and went finally to teach near Halifax, working, according to Charlotte, equally intolerable hours.[16] The Brontës' one break for freedom – their plan to establish a school of their own where, as Winnifrith remarks, 'they would not be subservient to anybody but where men of wealth would be subservient to them as they sent their daughters there'[17] – foundered for lack of capital and social contacts. All three women, then, were directly trapped in the educational machinery set up by the rich to exploit the sons and daughters of the 'genteel' poor; and this drastically tightened the social contradictions latent in their domestic context. Becoming a governess meant moving into a higher social circle, as well as a glad opportunity to exercise one's intellectual talents; but it also meant entering that desirable society precisely as a servant, as socially subservient to the very men and women to whom one felt culturally superior. The sisters moved physically into the class to which they 'spiritually' belonged – the cultivated society of Miss Branwell's nostalgic memories, the 'ancient family' of which Patrick spoke – only to suffer an acute sense of rejection and inferiority. Some of the families who employed them had remote but real connections with their own: Charlotte was for a time tutor to the daughters of the Sidgwicks, wealthy manufacturers who knew her somewhat, but Mrs Sidgwick simply ignored her. The crisis of self-division which this generated is clear enough in the Sidgwick family's comment that if they desired Charlotte to come to church with them she felt commanded like a slave, whereas if she were not invited she felt like an outcast dependant.[18] As Tom Winnifrith comments, 'In view of these links it is scarcely surprising that the sisters should have expected to have been treated like friends of the family, and it is scarcely surprising that when they were treated like governesses they felt bitterly hostile to the class which so despised them.'[19] Charlotte's two closest friends at Roe Head were Ellen Nussey, whose family, Tory to the core, had been local landowners for centuries, and Mary Taylor, daughter of a long-established radical, Nonconformist and feminist manufacturing family; yet these friendships gave her no entry to the circle of which the Nusseys and Taylors were part. (It is not difficult to see in that dual allegiance, experienced by Charlotte at a crucially formative moment, one source of that contention between the conflicting ideologies of conservative gentry and progressive bourgeoisie which provides a significant historical 'base' to her fiction.)

The Brontës' traumatic transition from the protected enclave of the parsonage, where exotic fantasy was allowed free rein, to the hard exigencies of a working world, has a representative rather than a purely personal significance. In that particular movement can be traced the shape of a more general historical phenomenon: that of the Romantic imagination being beaten down by society, stifled and shackled by mechanistic routine, hammering hopelessly at external limits.* It is a contradiction between imagination and society of which Charlotte herself was acutely aware: she writes in a letter to Ellen Nussey of the 'fiery imagination that at times eats me up and makes me feel society, as it *is*, wretchedly insipid. . . .'[20] The sisters' evangelical environment aggravated this contradiction: Evangelicalism is at once grimly hostile to the creative imagination and neurotically stimulant of frustrated fantasy. The Brontës' social isolation produced a similar effect, spurring the imagination to astonishing achievements but thrusting it back broodingly on itself in the absence of any fulfilling realisation.

In the Brontës' careers as governess, then, the historical frictions I have outlined were fleshed, realised and brought home as immediately personal experience. They felt, on the one hand, a fierce petty-bourgeois bitterness for those idle gentry whose pampered offspring they were required to enlighten; they experienced on the other hand a patronising distaste for the vulgar philistinism of the *nouveau riche*. Because they came of a professional rather than a commercial family they were able to feel culturally superior to the *arrivistes* around them; but that feeling was constantly shot through with a blunt, exasperated criticism of the traditional gentry which relates them to the plain, taciturn, hard-headed world of the old yeomanry and the new industrial capitalists.

---

* I do not mean to imply that the 'imagination' is some timeless positive value in itself; the opposition between 'imagination' and 'society', as the Brontës and other Romantics experienced it, is as it stands abstract and idealist.

We find in the Brontës, then, an abnormally stark opposition between a kind of 'pre-industrial' imaginative creativity, feeding off the resources of myth, archetype, rhetoric, melodrama, and the felt pressures of a drably spiritless society to which that imagination must either tortuously adapt or suffer extinction. Take, for example, the astonishing, tragicomic figure of the Brontës' brother, Branwell. Nothing could be easier than to read Branwell's doomed career in terms of some timeless Romantic archetype. Branwell, the self-taught translator of Horace, with his thirty-odd literary works scribbled between the ages of ten and seventeen, his moving, florid letters to Wordsworth and *Blackwood's Magazine*, his string of extravagant pseudonyms, his sketches of himself hanged and stabbed, his passion for boxing, his morose conviction of being eternally damned, his raffish carousals with failed artists in the George Hotel, Bradford: who could be more susceptible to a Romantic-individualist treatment? And yet the Branwell who began as a prolific contributor to the Angrian myths and ended as an embezzling ticket-clerk on Sowerby Bridge railway station was no mere historical eccentric. On the contrary, the tragedy of Branwell Brontë is a poignant symbol of a society in which imagination and reality could meet only in deadlock. Branwell, as Winifred Gerin has commented, was given by his father a Romantic education which completely unfitted him for industrial England;[21] his imagination was historically arrested, obsessionally fixated on heroic, military, traditionalist symbolism, on Wellington and Bonaparte. The 'Fall' from childhood mythology to social reality, the break which his sisters were forced to negotiate, proved in his case too much. Packed off to London with letters of introduction, launched as a painter of promise, he drank away his money in an East End boxers' pub, wandered about the metropolis in a dream, left his letters of introduction in his pocket and returned to Haworth with a pathetic tale of having been robbed. His impulsive and enthusiastic nature, Miss Gerin remarks, was 'frozen by the cold stare of the world',[22] and the comment seems just. Branwell's tragedy was by no means merely the story of any psychic cripple; through his impotence and inhibition speaks a whole epoch.

That the Brontë sisters were compelled in real life to negotiate the rift between 'imagination' and 'society' seems to me crucial for an understanding of their fiction. There was, on the one hand, the simple imperative to earn a living – the need for energy and drive, the respect for whatever was hardy, shrewd and stoical, the fellow-feeling for the victimised and dispossessed, the contempt for all that was pampered and parasitic. And yet, conversely, there was the admiration for that civilised delicacy which was where you spiritually belonged, a fascination with the genteel coupled with a distaste for the brash and pushing. That ambiguity was structural to the Brontës' social situation, estranged as they were at once from the rough life on their Haworth doorstep and the gentility in their neighbourhood. But I am claiming, too, that embodied in those personal deadlocks were wider historical conflicts, between the ideologies of landed gentry and bourgeoisie, which I have outlined as the 'deep structure' of the novels themselves. One particular complication within that structure is worth raising at this point. It is easy to see how the sisters' respect for the shrewd, hardy and energetic calls into play the identifiably bourgeois values of a progressive world; yet in a sense those values also refer nostalgically backwards, to the dour, settled milieu of the traditional Yorkshire yeomanry. Between these two classes in the West Riding there existed a certain community of sensibility; the yeomanry, like the radical Whig manufacturers, had traditionally a 'spirit of equality and republican independence'[23] which linked them in common antagonism to the conservative, jealousy exclusive and hierarchical gentry. The link, indeed, was more than one of sensibility: Mrs Gaskell points out how sections of the yeomanry in fact turned to manufacturing.[24] It is a cross-connection which will prove important in considering *Wuthering Heights*.

I have tried in this Introduction to outline both the method and intention of this book; and I should add that, for these to become fully apparent, the preliminary chapters on Charlotte's fiction should be taken together with the longer structural analysis of her novels which follows. Text, author, ideology, social class, productive forces: these are the terms I shall seek to bring together, by the mediatory concept of categorial structure. The aim of historical criticism is not to add specialist footnotes to literature; like any authentic criticism, its intention is to possess the work more deeply. To attend to the words on the page is excellent advice for a critic; all that needs to be added is that, unless we attend in that act to the history of which the words are the opaque but decipherable signs, we should not pretend that we are actually reading the work.

# 1 *Jane Eyre*

Helen Burns, the saintly schoolgirl of *Jane Eyre*, has an interestingly ambivalent attitude to the execution of Charles I. Discussing the matter with Jane, she thinks 'what a pity it was that, with his integrity and conscientiousness, he could see no farther than the prerogative of the crown. If he had but been able to look to a distance, and see to what they call the spirit of the age was tending! Still, I like Charles – I respect him – I pity him, poor murdered king! Yes, his enemies were the worst: they shed blood they had no right to shed. How dared they kill him!'[1]

Helen's curious vacillation between a coolly long-headed appreciation of essential reformist change and a spirited Romantic conservatism reflects a recurrent ambiguity in the novels of Charlotte Brontë. It is an ambiguity which shows up to some extent in Helen's own oppressed life at Lowood school: she herself, as a murdered innocent, is partly the martyred Charles, but unlike Charles she is also able to 'look to a distance' (although in her case towards heaven rather than future history), and counsel the indignant Jane in the virtues of patience and long-suffering. That patience implies both a 'rational' submission to the repressive conventions of Lowood (which she, unlike Jane, does not challenge), and a resigned endurance of life as a burden from which, in the end, will come release.

The problem which the novel faces here is how Helen's kind of self-abnegation is to be distinguished from the patently canting version of it offered by the sadistic Evangelical Brocklehurst, who justifies the eating of burnt porridge by an appeal to the torments of the early Christian martyrs. Submission is good, but only up to a point, and it is that point which Charlotte Brontë's novels explore, Jane's answer to Brocklehurst's enquiry as to how she will

avoid hell – 'I must keep in good health, and not die'² – mixes
childish naivety, cheek and seriousness: '*I* had no intention of
dying with him',³ she tells Rochester later. And indeed she doesn't:
it is mad Bertha who dies, leaving the way clear for Jane (who has
just refused St John Rivers's offer of premature death in India)
to unite with her almost martyred master. Helen Burns is a
necessary symbol, but her career is not to be literally followed.
When she smiles at the publicly chastised Jane in the Lowood
classroom, 'It was as if a martyr, a hero, had passed a slave or
victim, and imparted strength in the transit'.⁴ That conjunction of
'martyr' and 'hero' is significant: martyrdom is seen as both saintly
self-abnegation and heroic self-affirmation, a realisation of the self
through its surrender, as the name 'Burns' can signify both suffering and passion. But Helen, who fails to keep in good health and
dies, symbolises in the end only one aspect of this desirable
synthesis, that of passive renunciation. Like Jane, she triumphs
in the end over tyrannical convention, but unlike Jane that triumph
is achieved through her own death, not through someone else's.

Where Charlotte Brontë differs most from Emily is precisely
in this impulse to negotiate passionate self-fulfiment on terms
which preserve the social and moral conventions intact, and so
preserve intact the submissive, enduring, everyday self which
adheres to them. Her protagonists are an extraordinarily contradictory amalgam of smouldering rebelliousness and prim conventionalism, gushing Romantic fantasy and canny heard-headedness,
quivering sensitivity and blunt rationality. It is, in fact, a contradiction closely related to their roles as governesses or private tutors.
The governess is a servant, trapped within a rigid social function
which demands industriousness, subservience and self-sacrifice;
but she is also an 'upper' servant, and so (unlike, supposedly, other
servants) furnished with an imaginative awareness and cultivated
sensibility which are precisely her stock-in-trade as a teacher. She
lives at that ambiguous point in the social structure at which two
worlds – an interior one of emotional hungering, and an external
one of harshly mechanical necessity – meet and collide. At least,
they do collide if they are not wedged deliberately apart, locked
into their separate spheres to forestall the disaster of mutual in-
vasion. 'I seemed to hold two lives', says Lucy Snowe in *Villette*,
'the life of thought, and that of reality; and, provided the former

was nourished with a sufficiency of the strange necromantic joys of fancy, the privileges of the latter might remain limited to daily bread, hourly work, and a roof of shelter.'⁵ It is, indeed, with notable reluctance that Lucy is brought to confess the existence of an inner life at all: at the beginning of the novel she tells us, in a suspiciously overemphatic piece of assertion, that 'I, Lucy Snowe, plead guiltless of that curse, an overheated and discursive imagination'⁶ – and tells us this, moreover, in the context of an awed reference to ghostly haunting. Her response to the 'ghost' who flits through Madame Beck's garden is unwittingly comical in its clumsy lurching from romance to realism:

> Her shadow it was that tremblers had feared through long generations after her poor frame was dust; her black robe and white veil that, for timid eyes, moonlight and shade had mocked, as they fluctuated in the night-wind through the garden-thicket.
> Independently of romantic rubbish, however, that old garden had its charms. . . .⁷

It is a splitting of the self common in Charlotte's novels: Caroline Helstone in *Shirley* feels herself 'a dreaming fool', unfitted for 'ordinary intercourse with the ordinary world';⁸ and William Crimsworth of *The Professor*, slaving away as an underpaid clerk, finds little chance to prove that he is not 'a block, or a piece of furniture, but an acting, thinking, sentient man'.⁹

To allow passionate imagination premature rein is to be exposed, vulnerable and ultimately self-defeating: it is to be locked in the red room, enticed into bigamous marriage, ensnared like Caroline Helstone in a hopelessly self-consuming love. Passion springs from the very core of the self and yet is hostile, alien, invasive; the world of internal fantasy must therefore be locked away, as the mad Mrs Rochester stays locked up on an upper floor of Thornfield, slipping out to infiltrate the 'real' world only in a few unaware moments of terrible destructiveness. The inner world must yield of necessity to the practical virtues of caution, tact and observation espoused by William Crimsworth – the wary, vigilant virtues by which the self's lonely integrity can be defended in a spying, predatory society, a society on the watch for the weak spot which will surrender you into its hands. The Romantic self must be persistently recalled to its deliberately narrowed and withered definition of rationality. 'Order! No snivel! – no sentiment! – no regret! I will endure only sense and resolution',[10] whispers Jane Eyre to herself, fixing her errant thoughts on the hard fact that her relationship with Rochester is of a purely cash-nexus kind. In the end, of course, it isn't. With the ambiguous exception of *Villette*, the strategy of the novels is to allow the turbulent inner life satisfying realisation without that self-betraying prematureness which would disrupt the self's principled continuity – a continuity defined by its adherence to a system of social and moral convention. The tactic most commonly employed here is the conversion of submissive conventionalism itself from a mode of self-preservation to a mode of conscious or unconscious self-advancement. Mrs Reed's remark to Jane in the red room – 'It is only on condition of perfect submission and stillness that I shall liberate you'[11] – is triumphantly validated by the novel: it is Jane's stoical Quakerish stillness which captivates Rochester. Her refusal to act prematurely for her own ends both satisfies restrictive convention and leads ultimately to a fulfilling transcendence of it. Rochester would not of course find Jane attractive if she were merely dull, but neither would he love her if, like Blanche Ingram, she were consciously after his money. Jane must therefore reveal enough repressed, Blanche-like 'spirit' beneath her puritan exterior to stimulate and cajole him, without any suggestion that she is, in Lucy Snowe's revealing words about herself, 'bent on success'. Jane manages this difficult situation adroitly during their courtship, blending flashes of flirtatious self-assertion with her habitual meek passivity; she sees shrewdly that 'a lamb-like submission and turtle-dove sensibility' would end by boring him. She must demonstrate her quietly self-sufficient independence of Rochester as a way of keeping him tied to her, and so, paradoxically, of staying tied to and safely dependent on him. That this involves a good deal of dexterous calculation – calculation which, if pressed too far, would seriously undermine Jane's credibility as a character – should be obvious enough: it is not, perhaps, wholly insignificant that Rochester's comment to Jane in the original manuscript – 'coin one of your wild, shy, provoking smiles' – is misprinted in the first edition as 'wild, *sly*, provoking smiles'. If Rochester recognises Jane intuitively as a soul-mate, so after all does St John Rivers, who tells her that his ambition is unlimited, his desire to rise higher insatiable, and his favoured virtues 'endurance, perseverance, industry, talent'.[12] Rivers must of course be rejected, as reason rather than feeling is his guide, and Jane's career can only culminate successfully when 'feeling' can be 'rationally' released; feeling without judgement, she muses, is 'a washy draught indeed', but judgement without feeling is 'too bitter and husky a morsel for human deglutition'.[13] Even so, there is more than a superficial relationship between Rivers, a rationalist with feverishly repressed impulses, and Jane's own behaviour: in her case, too, 'Reason sits firm and holds the reins, and she will not let the feelings burst away and hurry her to wild chasms'.[14] Not prematurely, anyway, and certainly not to early death in India.

Jane, then, must refuse Rivers as she has refused Rochester: loveless conventionalism and illicit passion both threaten the kind of fulfilment the novel seeks for her. Yet of course Rivers represents more than mere convention. In his fusion of disciplined aloofness and restless desire he is an extreme version of Jane herself, akin to her in more than blood; and he is acute enough to spot the affinity: 'for in your nature is an alloy as detrimental to repose as that in mine; though of a different kind'.[15] The difference, however, is what finally counts. It is true that Jane finds Rivers's restlessness intriguing as well as alarming: the 'frequent flash and changeful dilation of his eye',[16] his 'troubling impulses of insatiate yearnings and disquieting aspirations',[17] evoke crucial aspects of herself at the same time as they recall Rochester's engaging moodiness. Indeed, Rivers's repressed love for Rosamund Oliver is a cruder, more agonised version of Rochester's own early enigmatic relationship with Jane. Yet Rivers is a frigid as well as a Romantic figure, and for Jane to accept him would mean disastrous compromise. 'I daily wished more to please him: but to do so, I felt daily more and more that I must disown half my nature, stifle half my faculties, wrest my tastes from their original bent, force myself to the adoption of pursuits for which I had no natural vocation.'[18]

Half her nature is significant. Rivers is not to be dismissed out of hand, since like Rochester he images aspects of Jane's fractured self which must not be denied. Both men are also attractive in a more subtle sense: each lives out a different kind of deadlock between passion and convention, suffering and affirmation, and so projects Jane's own predicament in more dramatic style. Rochester, an oppressed younger son of the gentry, has suffered at the hands of social convention and so like Jane has a history of deprivation; but unlike her he has achieved worldly success, cuts a glamorous figure in county society, and so blends social desirability with a spice of thwarted passion and an underdog past. His cool attempt to violate the marriage conventions suggests a cavalier stance towards the code which governs Jane, and so, while naturally condemned by her, displays the flamboyant mastery she finds alluring in him because it is absent in herself. At the same time, however, his bigamous scheme is a pathetically abortive rebellion against the stringent pressures of orthodoxy, and so stirs Jane's sympathetic fellow-feeling. The act confirms his superiority to Jane while showing what they have in common, brings him within emotional reach without damage to the dominative style which makes him worth reaching for. Rivers, by contrast, is unconventional in his moral absolutism but socially tame; unlike Rochester's sexual energy, his abstract passion can easily be contained within the social code which limits companionship between the sexes to marriage. He is, indeed, unconventional only because he presses the orthodox view that duty must conquer feeling to a parodic extreme; and in this he is a peculiarly pure image of the ideology which victimises Jane, as his affinities with Brocklehurst would suggest. Even so, because Rivers forces Brocklehurst's ideology to a pitch of Romantic intensity, he seems to offer Jane a version of what she finally achieves with Rochester: a way of conforming to convention which at the same time draws you beyond it, gathers you into a fuller, finer self-realisation. The point is that such a resolution is available in India for Rivers, but not for Jane. Rivers the missionary is both martyr and hero; Jane would merely have been a martyr.

In so far as Rivers's twisted heroism mixes hard-headed ambition with a touch of Romance, it has its ambiguous appeal to Jane. His detection of kindred impulses in her is shrewd: she has hardly arrived at Thornfield before she is climbing to the leads and scanning the skyline, longing 'for a power of vision which might overpass that limit; which might reach the busy world, towns, regions full of life I had heard of but never seen. . . .'[19] But Jane's ambition can be assuaged, as Rivers's cannot be. The popu-

lous horizons she scans are soon made incarnate in the well-
travelled figure of Rochester, brought within the domestic confines
of Thornfield to license an equable balance of settlement and
stimulation, the foreign and the familiar. Unlike the lower, more
provincially-minded gentry, the class to which Rochester belongs is
at once local and cosmopolitan, equally at home in the great house
and the great world. It is true that Rochester himself feels at home
in neither: Thornfield means mad Bertha, and travelling is merely
a desperate way of evading her memory. Yet Rochester as Romantic ideal unites Jane's brooding desire for love and security with
her eager extraversion to the busy realm of action, the aura of
which still glows around her world-weary master. 'Romanticism'
in Charlotte's fiction commonly has this dual meaning: it signifies
the active, worldly, expansive self, but also the conservative impulse
to withdraw protectively into some idealised enclave. If Rochester
has the edge over Rivers it is partly because he can meet both
demands together; Rivers can satisfy only the first.

Rivers's demands, indeed, pull in precisely the opposite direction to Rochester's. He threatens to uproot you lovelessly from
idyllic settlement to an *unpleasantly* foreign world, and to a life
with no determinate end but death. Jane is certainly willing at
times to trade settlement for independence: much as she finds the
soft domesticity of the Rivers girls seductive, she is quick to tell
St John that she wants an income of her own. In India, however,
she would have the worst of all worlds: homelessness, loveless-
ness and subjugation. She rejects Rivers not only because his
demands violate her identity, but because of his imperious masculinity. In India she would be 'at his side always, and always re-
strained, and always checked -- forced to keep the fire of [her]
nature continually low, to compel it to burn inwardly and never
utter a cry, though the imprisoned flame consume vital after
vital'.[20] Far from combining the excitingly exotic with the lovably
familiar, India for Jane would be a mixture of the alien and the
over-close. Charlotte's heroines, as we shall see, habitually welcome
male domination as a stimulant to their fiery natures; but Rivers's
despotism would be merely oppressive. Jane, then, is willing to
accompany him to India if she may go free: 'I will give the missionary my energies – it is all he wants – but not myself: that
would be only adding the husk and shell to the kernel. For them

he has no use: I retain them'.[21] Scathingly inverting the husk –
kernel image, Jane accepts the social role of missionary only if she
can preserve unbetrayed the authentic self which belongs to
Rochester; and this is hardly a constructive advance on the
schizoid condition she has endured for most of her life. Rivers
offers a social function which involves the sacrifice of personal
fulfilment; Rochester's offer involves exactly the opposite. Both
are inferior propositions to becoming Mrs Rochester, at once a
fulfilling personal commitment and an enviable public role.

Like Charlotte's other protagonists, Jane does not regard labour
as an end in itself. Will and hard work are important, but they must
finally culminate in an achieved repose inimical to Rivers's nature.
William Crimsworth of *The Professor* is as resolutely single-
minded as Rivers in his pursuit of desirable ends, but he knows
when to stop: having made his fortune in Europe he retires to
England as a gentleman of leisure. With Rivers, however, there
is no end to enterprise, as Diana warns Jane: 'Think of the task
you undertook – one of incessant fatigue: where fatigue kills even
the strong; and you are weak. St John – you know him – would
urge you to impossibilities: with him there would be no permission to rest during the hot hours; and unfortunately, I have
noticed, whatever he exacts, you force yourself to perform.'[22]
Rivers's goals are of course spiritual, and Crimsworth's material;
but the parallel is surely as significant as the contrast. Rivers is
a spiritual bourgeois eager to reap inexhaustible profits, un-
flaggingly devoted to the purchase of souls. His driving will,
rigorous self-discipline and fear of emotional entanglements reveal
well enough the analogy between Evangelical and entrepreneur.
Indeed, Rivers himself candidly admits the connection, if not
exactly in those terms. His evangelical zeal is a sublimation of
thwarted worldly impulse:

A year ago I was myself intensely miserable, because I thought
I had made a mistake in entering the ministry: its uniform
duties wearied me to death. I burnt for the more active life of
the world – for the more exciting toils of a literary career –
for the destiny of an artist, author, orator; anything, rather
than that of a priest: yes, the heart of a politician, of a soldier,
of a votary of glory, a lover of renown, a luster after power, beat

under my curate's surplice. I considered; my life was so
wretched, it must be changed, or I must die. After a season of
darkness and struggling, light broke and relief fell: my cramped
existence all at once spread out to a plain without bounds –
my powers heard a call from heaven to rise, gather their full
strength, spread their wings and mount beyond ken. God had
an errand for me; to bear which afar, to deliver it well, skill and
strength, courage and eloquence, the best qualifications of
soldier, statesman and orator were all needed: for these all
centre in the good missionary.[28]

The similarity with Jane's own frustrated condition is notable,
but so too is the difference. Rivers can gain a taste of mundane
glory only by embracing danger, obscurity and premature death;
Jane moves in the opposite direction, away from obscurity to
a success which is at once secure, emotionally fulfilling and, in the
world's eyes, highly desirable. In one sense Rivers is too worldly
for Jane, trampling ambitiously over the values of cloistered
domestic love; in another sense he is not worldly enough, fanatic-
ally prepared to squander his life in a remote society. Like Helen
Burns, he signifies a perspective which it is vital to acknowledge
but perilous to take literally; and the fact that the novel allows
him the last word reflects its uneasiness about the victory to which
it brings Jane. Rivers at least, the final paragraphs seem to proclaim,
has not temporised between the competing claims of world and
spirit, whereas the novel has indeed negotiated such a compromise
on behalf of its heroine.
  Yet the uneasiness is strictly qualified, not least because of the
disparity between the final pious phrase ('Amen; even so come,
Lord Jesus!') and the man we knew, whose self-denial was
guiltily entwined with thrusting self-assertion. Rivers *has* temporised between world and spirit, even if we are now asked to
forget the fact and revere him as an image of saintly self-surrender.
Even that reverence, however, has its limits: Rivers is introduced
into the novel just as Jane has made a painfully authentic self-
sacrifice, in order to dramatise the dangers inherent in that virtue
and so pave the way back to Rochester and life. Jane flippantly
denies that her return to Rochester involves any sort of martyrdom
('Sacrifice! What do I sacrifice? Famine for food, expectation for

B

content'²⁴), and of course she is right; but besides forestalling our own mixed feelings about Jane's fairy-tale triumph by saying it for us, the comment is meant to alert us to the real deprivations she has endured, and so obviate any sense that she has won her self-fulfilment on the cheap. Jane and Rochester are also martyrs in their own successful way; and in this sense the final unbanishable image of Rivers is less a critique of their conjugal happiness than a symbol of the suffering they underwent to achieve it – the patron saint, as it were, of the marriage. It is convenient to leave Rivers with the last word when the genuine threat he represents has been nullified.

Authentic though Jane's renunciation of Rochester is, it has much in common with Rivers's egoistic self-sacrifice to the missionary cause:

> Feeling . . . clamoured wildly. 'Oh, comply!' it said. Think of his misery; think of his danger – look at his state when left alone. . . . Who in the world cares for *you?* or who will be injured by what you do?'
> Still indomitable was the reply – '*I* care for myself. The more solitary, the more friendless, the more unsustained I am, the more I will respect myself. I will keep the law given by God; sanctioned by man. . . .'²⁵

Jane responds similarly to St John's sneer that she refuses his offer because she is afraid of death. 'I am. God did not give me my life to throw away; and to do as you wish me would, I begin to think, be almost equivalent to committing suicide.'²⁶ For someone as socially isolated as Jane, the self is all one has; and it is not to be recklessly invested in dubious enterprises. 'Self-possession' comes to assume a meaning deeper than the coolly impenetrable composure it signifies in all Charlotte's novels: it suggests also a nurturing and hoarding of the self, a prudent refusal to yield it prematurely in ways which might lead to rash dissipation rather than to increase and enrichment. It is a sense of the self which springs in part from the condition of orphanage. Like almost all of Charlotte's protagonists, Jane is stripped from the outset of significant ties of kin; the self is less a relational reality than a watchful, alien presence on the periphery of others' lives. 'You have no business to take our books', John Reed tells her; 'you are a dependant, mamma says; you have no money; your father left you none; you ought to beg, and not to live here with gentlemen's children like us, and eat the same meals we do, and wear clothes at our mamma's expense.'[27] For John Reed, who you are is a function of your role within a defined system of kinship; for an orphaned outsider like Jane, identity is at once dependent on and denied by one's relatives. It is this which is at the root of her terror and estrangement, as an 'uncongenial alien permanently intruded on [Mrs Reed's] family';[28] she feels secure only when a stranger enters the room. But if orphanage abandons the self to solitude, it also releases it into freedom. 'I am glad you are no relation of mine', Jane cries defiantly to Mrs Reed, and looking at what happens to the Reed family one can see her point. That cloyingly permissive world, cohered in part by the violence it wreaks on the scapegoat alien, leads to dissipation in John, emotional withering in Eliza, witless frivolity in Georgiana and premature death for the harassed mother. The Reed family is a nexus of conflict which Jane is indeed well out of; her later return to Gateshead demonstrates how well she has prospered by independent effort and how little she needs them – how much, in a satisfying inversion of the power-relationship, they now need her. To be bereft of relations is pitiable, but breaking ties proves exhilarating: after her scorching denunciation of Mrs Reed, 'my soul began to expand, to exult, with the strangest sense of freedom, of triumph, I ever felt. It seemed as if an invisible bond had burst, and that I had struggled out into unhoped-for liberty.'[29] Liberty and alienation are closely linked, as Jane implies when Rochester wonders prophetically whether anyone will meddle with their marriage arrangements: 'There is no one to meddle, sir. I have no kindred to interfere.'[30] Rochester is less fortunate than Jane in this respect: it is his interfering kinsman who wrecks his plans. Being alone entails the bondage of earning your living unsupported, but unshackles you from inherited duties into relative mobility; if there is nobody to love you there is equally nobody to hold you back. It is an ambiguity illustrated in Jane's response to leaving Lowood: she is uncertain how far severing that bond involves freedom or servitude. Leaving school means venturing into a world whose very threats seem enthralling: 'I remembered that the real world was wide, and that a varied field of hopes and fears, of sensations and excitements, awaited those who had courage to go forth into its expanse, to seek real knowledge of life amidst its perils.'[31] But the buoyancy of the enterprising in- dividualist with the world at her feet is immediately deflated. Jane's prayers for liberty, and then – rationally paring down her hubristic demands – for at least 'change and stimulus', are scattered to the winds; in the end she settles glumly for 'at least a new servitude'. All the oppressed self can finally affirm is a refresh- ingly novel kind of passivity.

At the centre of all Charlotte's novels, I am arguing, is a figure who either lacks or deliberately cuts the bonds of kinship. This leaves the self a free, blank, 'pre-social' atom: free to be injured and exploited, but free also to progress, move through the class-structure, choose and forge relationships, strenuously utilise its talents in scorn of autocracy or paternalism. The novels are deeply informed by this bourgeois ethic, but there is more to be said than that. For the social status finally achieved by the *dé- raciné* self is at once meritoriously won and inherently proper. Jane's uncle is said to be a tradesman, and the Reeds despise her for it; but Bessie comments that the Eyres were as much gentry as the Reeds, and her Rivers cousins have an impressively ancient lineage. Rochester seems a grander form of gentry, and Jane's relationship with him is of course socially unequal; but it is, never- theless, a kind of returning home as well as an enviable move upwards. Given relationships are certainly constrictive: they mediate a suave violence deep-seated in society itself, as John Reed's precociously snobbish remark suggests. But knowing where you genetically belong still counts for a good deal in the end. Charlotte's fiction portrays the unprotected self in its lonely con- quest of harsh conditions, and so intimates a meritocratic vision; but individualist self-reliance leads you to roles and relations which are objectively fitting.

Jane, then, disowns what second-hand kin she has, caring never to see the Reeds again, surviving instead by her own talents; she creates the relationships which matter, those of spiritual rather than blood affinity. ('I believe [Rochester] is of mine; – I am sure he is, – I feel akin to him . . . though rank and wealth sever us widely, I have something in my brain and heart, in my blood and nerves, that assimilates me mentally to him.'[32] Spiritual affinity, indeed, is more physical and full-blooded than the icy *rapport* one has with literal kinsfolk like Rivers. In this as in other ways, however, Jane is granted the best of both worlds. Just as her resources for solitary survival run out, on the long exhausting flight from Thornfield, she is supplied with a new set of kinsfolk who turn out this time to be pleasant. The Rivers sisters provide a cultivated retreat into which Jane can temporarily relax; she rests her head on Diana's lap in delighted gratitude at her discovery of blood-relations, even though the event will prove merely a stopping-off place *en route* to the grander gentility of Rochester. This time, however, her relation to kinsfolk is not that of servile dependence. On the contrary, it is they who are now in part dependent on her: each of them gets a quarter share of her newfound wealth. The legacy allows Jane to combine sturdy independence with a material sealing of her affinity with others. Given relationships are good, if you may negotiate them on your own terms; kinsmen are both gift and threat. It is an ambivalence reflected in Jane's feelings towards Mrs Reed: she upbraids her hotly for neglecting familial duty, but curiously excuses that brutality by wondering 'how could she really like an interloper not of her race, and unconnected with her, after her husband's death, by any tie?'[33] Whether 'race' matters or not seems a moot point in Jane's own mind.

Jane's relative isolation from given relationships results in a proud autonomy of spirit, one which in some ways implicitly questions the class-structure. She has too much self-respect to lavish her love on an unresponsive Rochester: 'He is not of your order; keep to your caste; and be too self-respecting to lavish the love of the whole heart, soul, and strength, where such a gift is not wanted and may be despised.'[34] Yet the comment, of course, endorses the class-structure as well as suggesting the spiritual inferiority of one's betters: if the callously insensitive aristocrat cannot recognise a gift when he sees one, then it is wise to remain self-righteously on one's own side of the social divide. In so far as it is for him to make the overture, Jane's attitude combines deference with independence; yet 'independence' is a thoroughly ambiguous term. It means not wanting to be a servant, which implies a class-judgement on those below you as well as suggesting a radical attitude to those above. Jane's rebellion against the Reeds

engages certain egalitarian feelings: she rejects the idea of paternalist benefaction as disagreeable, and later values her equal relationship with Mrs Fairfax for the freedom it brings. 'The equality
between her and me was real; not the mere result of condescension
on her part; so much the better – my position was all the freer.'[35]
But independence in this society involves attaining a precarious
gentility (Bessie has to admit that the adult Jane is now, at least,
a lady), and that in turn entails a sharp eye for the nuance of
social distinction. Jane is furious with the Reeds because they
treat her as a servant when she isn't one; her smouldering hatred
of their snobbery is thus shot through with shared class-assump-
tions about the poor. ('No; I should not like to belong to poor
people.'[36]) Her response to the pupils at Morton school is similarly
double-edged: distasteful though she finds their unmannerliness,
she 'must not forget that these coarsely-clad little peasants are of
flesh and blood as good as the scions of the gentlest genealogy;
and that the germs of native excellence, refinement, intelligence,
kind feeling, are as likely to exist in their hearts as in those of the
best born'.[37] The demotic generosity of this is sharply qualified
by that stern self-reminder; Jane's doctrine of spiritual equality
stems logically from her own experience, but it has to fight hard
against the social discriminations bred into an expensively clad
child. (Her egalitarian defence of the 'British peasantry' is based,
ironically, on a dogma of chauvinist superiority: they are at least
preferable to their 'ignorant, coarse, and besotted' European
counterparts.) Jane feels degraded by her role as schoolmistress
('I had taken a step which sank instead of raising me in the scale
of social existence'[38]), but guiltily scorns the feeling as 'idiotic';
and that tension deftly defines the petty-bourgeois consciousness
which clings to real class-distinctions while spiritually rejecting
them. She is, for instance, priggishly quick to point out to the
Rivers' servant Hannah that she may be a beggar but at least she
is a high-class one:

'Are you book-learned?' [Hannah] inquired, presently.
'Yes, very.'[39]

The snobbish Hannah must be given an object-lesson in social
equality, taught not to judge by appearances, so Jane reveals how
superior she is to the old woman. Even in beggary class counts:

St John Rivers, presumably noting Jane's refined accent when
Hannah turns her from his door, surmises instantly that this is
a 'peculiar case'.[40] Jane's insistence on getting past the servant
and appealing to the young ladies glimpsed within is, indeed,
sound class tactics: the sisters are presented as idealised versions
of herself, quiet, spiritual and self-composed.

Jane's relationship with Rochester is marked by these ambiguities of equality, servitude and independence. He himself conceives
of the union in terms of spiritual equality: ' "My bride is here",
he said, again drawing me to him, "because my equal is here, and
my likeness. Jane, will you marry me?" '[41] Far from offering a
radically alternative ethic, spiritual equality is what actually
smooths your progress through the class-system; Rochester may
be spiritually egalitarian but he is still socially eligible. Jane is on
the whole submissive to social hierarchy but shares her master's
view that spiritual qualities count for more: she has no hesitation in dismissing Blanche Ingram as inferior to herself. She wants
a degree of independence in marriage – ' "It would indeed be a
relief", I thought, "if I had ever so small an independency" '[42] –
but it is, significantly, 'small': she can hope to bring Rochester an
accession of fortune but hardly to get on genuinely equal terms.
Independence, then, is an intermediate position between complete
equality and excessive docility: it allows you freedom, but freedom within a proper deference.

When stung to righteous anger, Jane can certainly claim a
fundamental human equality with her employer: 'Do you think,
because I am poor, obscure, plain, and little, I am soulless and
heartless?'[43] There are, in fact, reasons other than simple humani-
tarian ones why Jane and Rochester are not as socially divided as
may at first appear. Rochester, the younger son of an avaricious
landed gentleman, was denied his share in the estate and had to
marry instead into colonial wealth; Jane's colonial uncle dies and
leaves her a sizeable legacy, enough for independence. The colonial
trade which signified a decline in status for Rochester signifies
an advance in status for Jane, so that although they are of course
socially unequal, their fortunes spring from the same root. Yet
Jane does not finally claim equality with Rochester; the primary
terms on which Charlotte Brontë's fiction handles relationships
are those of dominance and submission. The novels dramatise a

society in which almost all human relationships are power-struggles; and because 'equality' therefore comes to be defined as equality of power, it is an inevitably complicated affair. Jane serves in the end 'both for [Rochester's] prop and guide',⁴⁴ which is an interestingly ambiguous situation. It suggests subservience, and so perpetuates their previous relationship; but the subservience is also, of course, a kind of leadership. Whether she likes it or not, Jane finally comes to have power over Rochester. Her ultimate relation to him is a complex blend of independence (she comes to him on her own terms, financially self-sufficient), submissiveness, and control.

This complex blend is a recurrent feature of relationships in the novels. Charlotte's protagonists want independence, but they also desire to dominate; and their desire to dominate is matched only by their impulse to submit to a superior will. The primary form assumed by this ambiguity is a sexual one: the need to venerate and revere, but also to exercise power, enacts itself both in a curious rhythm of sexual attraction and antagonism, and in a series of reversals of sexual roles. The maimed and blinded Rochester, for example, is in an odd way even more 'masculine' than he was before (he is 'brown', 'shaggy', 'metamorphosed into a lion'), but because he is helpless he is also 'feminine';* and Jane, who adopts a traditionally feminine role towards him ('It is time some one undertook to rehumanise you'⁴⁵), is thereby forced into the male role of protectiveness. She finds him both attractive and ugly, as he finds her both plain and fascinating. Rochester's lack of conventional good looks, in contrast to Rivers's blandly classical features, reflects his idiosyncratic roughness and so underlines his male mastery, but it also makes him satisfyingly akin to Jane herself. Blanche Ingram is a 'beauty', but her aggressive masculinity contrasts sharply with Jane's pale subduedness; her dominative nature leads her to desire a husband who will be a foil rather

---

* A sexual ambiguity prefigured in Rochester's masquerading as an old gypsy woman. Then he was a masculine female, now he is a feminine male. The gypsy image occurs early in the novel in the song Bessie sings to Jane, as an image of the unorthodox freedom of those so low in the class-structure as to be effectively 'outside' it; it is used similarly of Heathcliff in *Wuthering Heights*. Its association with Rochester seems appropriate: he is both unconventional and 'free' of the class-structure in the peculiar sense in which those who control it are.

than a rival to her, but it also prompts her to despise effeminate men and admire strong ones:

> 'I grant an ugly *woman* is a blot on the fair face of creation; but as to the *gentlemen*, let them be solicitous to possess only strength and valour: let their motto be: — Hunt, shoot and fight: the rest is not worth a fillip. Such should be my device, were I a man.'
> 'Whenever I marry,' she continued, after a pause which none interrupted, 'I am resolved my husband shall not be a rival, but a foil to me. I will suffer no competitor near the throne; I shall exact an undivided homage; his devotions shall not be shared between me and the shape he sees in his mirror.'[46]

The arrogance of this, of course, counts heavily against Blanche; it is hardly likely to charm the listening Rochester. Jane, who shares Blanche's liking for 'devilish' men, knows better than she does how they are to be handled — when to exert her piquant will and when to be cajolingly submissive:

> I knew the pleasure of vexing and soothing him by turns; it was one I chiefly delighted in, and a sure instinct always prevented me from going too far: beyond the verge of provocation I never ventured; on the extreme brink I liked well to try my skill. Retaining every minute form of respect, every propriety of my station, I could still meet him in argument without fear or uneasy restraint: this suited both him and me.[47]

Jane moves deftly between male and female roles in her courtship of Rochester; unlike Blanche, who is tall, dark and dominating like Rochester himself, she settles astutely for a vicarious expression of her own competitive maleness through him. She preserves the proprieties while turning them constantly to her advantage, manipulating convention for both self-protection and self-advancement.

This simultaneity of attraction and antagonism, reverence and dominance, is relevant to a more general ambiguity about power which pervades Charlotte's fiction. It parallels and embodies the conflicting desires of the oppressed outcast for independence, for passive conformity to a secure social order, and for avenging self-assertion over that order. Revenge does not, in fact, seem too strong a word for what happens at the end of *Jane Eyre*. Jane's repressed indignation at a dominative society, prudently swallowed back throughout the book, is finally released – not by Jane herself, but by the novelist; and the victim is the symbol of that social order, Rochester. The crippled Rochester is the novel's sacrificial offering to social convention, to Jane's subconscious hostility and, indeed, to her own puritan guilt; by satisfying all three demands simultaneously, it allows her to adopt a suitably subjugated role while experiencing a fulfilling love and a taste of power. Jane's guilt about Rochester's passion and her own is strikingly imaged in the grotesque figure of Bertha: the Bertha who tries on Jane's wedding veil is a projection of Jane's sexually tormented subconsciousness, but since Bertha is masculine, black-visaged and almost the same height as her husband, she appears also as a repulsive symbol of Rochester's sexual drive. The point of the novel's conclusion is to domesticate that drive so that it ceases to be minatory while remaining attractive. In the end, the outcast bourgeoise achieves more than a humble place at the fireside: she also gains independence vis-à-vis the upper class, and the right to engage in the process of taming it. The worldly Rochester has already been purified by fire; it is now for Jane to rehumanise him. By the device of an ending, bourgeois initiative and genteel settlement, sober rationality and Romantic passion, spiritual equality and social distinction, the actively affirmative and the patiently deferential self, can be merged into mythical unity.

# 2 The Professor

St John Rivers's bourgeois values of 'endurance, perseverance, industry, talent',[1] if sinisterly unfeeling in Jane Eyre's eyes, are certainly shared by William Crimsworth of *The Professor*, whose motto, suitably, is 'Hope smiles on effort'. Yet Crimsworth is not a middle-class philistine but a feminine, sensitive soul, too delicately cultivated to endure the deadeningly oppressive clerical work to which his manufacturing brother Edward sets him. He is despised by Edward and jocularly scorned by the radical, sardonic Whig capitalist Hunsden; yet his progress through the novel involves an interesting inversion of his original victimised condition. Crimsworth's mother was an aristocrat and his father a manufacturer; but whereas the callous Edward has inherited, temperamentally, only from his father, Crimsworth has been conveniently engrafted with qualities from both parents, and the combination proves unbeatable. He is superior in imaginative sensibility to both Edward and Hunsden (who hates poetry), and it is this trait which, as with Jane Eyre and Lucy Snowe, brings him at first to suffer degradation at the hands of a crassly authoritarian society. But it is also the quality which, combined with a quietly industrious knack of amassing a little capital through years of 'bustle, action, unslacked endeavour',[2] allows him to prosper as a private teacher and return to England as a gentleman of leisure. Crimsworth is able to make classic bourgeois progress – not, however, on the crudely materialist terms of his brother, but in ways which utilise rather than negate his 'genteel' accomplishments. He reproduces the fusion of aristocratic quality and driving bourgeois effort effected in his parents' marriage, but does so in more propitious conditions: his mother had been disowned by her family for marrying beneath her.

*The Professor* is essentially a more dishonest and idealised
version of *Jane Eyre* and *Villette*. As the choice of a male protagonist suggests, it is concerned with the victory rather than the
vulnerability of the solitary social aspirant, and so represses whole
dimensions of agony apparent in the other two works. Crimsworth's desire to enter trade may be a lonely rebellion against
intolerable aristocratic patronage ('such was the scorn in Lord
Tynedale's countenance as he pronounced the word *trade* . . . that
I was instantly decided'³), but it is at least a free choice, rather
than, as with Jane and Lucy, an unavoidable fatality. The option
has a generational logic about it ('I cannot do better than follow
in my father's footsteps'⁴), but its rash arbitrariness has a grandly
existentialist flavour too: 'you have chosen trade, and you shall
be a tradesman'.⁵ Rejecting the burdensome kinship of the Seacombes, Crimsworth becomes a solitary agent in search of a role,
blankly selecting a commitment: 'yes, I will be a tradesman'.⁶
His ignorance of his chosen vocation is alarming – he doesn't even
know that rich manufacturers tend to live outside the towns
where they conduct their business – but even his ignorance has a
faint touch of aristocratic *panache* about it. The gratuitousness of
his commitment lays him open to Hunsden's needling satire, but
at the same time idealises the forced labour of the Brontë sisters;
it displays the spirited self-reliance which will pull him through,
with fewer pitfalls to face than Lucy or Jane.
   Crimsworth is understandably resentful that Edward refuses to
acknowledge their blood-tie, but he is also grateful to be ignored:

> . . . hear once and for all what I have to say about our relation-
> ship, and all that sort of humbug! I must have no nonsense on
> that point; it would never suit me. I shall excuse you nothing on
> the plea of being my brother; if I find you stupid, negligent,
> dissipated, idle, or possessed of any faults detrimental to the
> interests of the house, I shall dismiss you as I would any other
> clerk. . . . Do you understand?'
>    'Partly', I replied. 'I suppose you mean that I am to do my
> work for my wages; not to expect favour from you, and not to
> depend on you for any help but what I earn; that suits me
> exactly, and on these terms I will consent to be your clerk.'⁷

As in *Jane Eyre*, isolation from kinsfolk ensures independence, so that Crimsworth is able slyly to invert the power-relationship in his final phrase, graciously consenting to become Edward's wage-slave. Yet, again like *Jane Eyre*, blood still counts for much. Crimsworth is a genetic blend of bourgeois enterprise and aristocratic grace; and it is these inherited characteristics which allow him to rebel successfully against the Seacombes on the one hand and Edward on the other. If he is roused to instinctive defiance by the aristocracy's snobbish anti-commercialism, he also has enough upper-class trust in his own spiritual superiority to cope with his boorish brother. 'Had I been in anything inferior to him, he would not have hated me so thoroughly, but I knew all that he knew, and, what was worse, he suspected that I kept a padlock of silence on mental wealth in which he was no sharer.' [8] (Whether that financial metaphor is an ironic gibe at Edward or a revealing index of Crimsworth's own imagination is left ambiguous.) As the feeble aristocrat of the family, Crimsworth may not be physically 'as fine a fellow as [his] plebeian brother by a long chalk',[9] but even physically he resembles him, as a kind of inferior model: 'In face I resembled him, though I was not so handsome; my features were less regular; I had a darker eye, and a broader brow – in form I was greatly inferior – thinner, slighter, not so tall.'[10] Crimsworth is in the end a smaller entrepreneur than his brother too, but the family resemblance shows up here as well.

Crimsworth also compares himself physically with Yorke Hunsden, his scourge and *alter ego*:

I employed the interval of silence in a rapid scrutiny of his physiognomy. I had never observed him closely before; and, as my sight is very short, I had gathered only a vague, general idea of his appearance; I was surprised now, on examination, to perceive how small, and even feminine, were his lineaments; his tall figure, long and dark locks, his voice and general bearing, had impressed me with the notion of something powerful and massive; not at all: – my own features were cast in a harsher and squarer mould than his. I discerned that there would be contrasts between his inward and outward man; contentions, too: for I suspected his soul had more of will and ambition than his body had of fibre and muscle.[11]

Crimsworth, as a sort of male Jane Eyre, habitually plays a feminine
role to Hunsden's Rochester, so it is pleasurable to find the relation reversed on closer inspection. William now stands to Hunsden
almost as Edward stands to himself; the plainness which renders
Crimsworth inferior to his brother also makes him seem tougher
than Hunsden. This gives the Professor an enjoyable mental edge
over the man who dominates him, without actually disrupting their
inequality; yet Hunsden's femininity (his face, Crimsworth muses,
would produce the same effect on a woman as an interesting female
face would on a man) serves conversely to equalise the relationship
somewhat, since Crimsworth is hardly virile himself. Hunsden's
inner contention of soul and body also reveals his affinities with
William who, like all of Charlotte's protagonists, displays at the
outset a severe disjunction between mind and material circumstance; but since the novel handles this aspect of William with
notable externality, concerned as it is to spotlight his strengths
rather than his flaws, we are left, here too, with a sense of his
superiority to Hunsden. Crimsworth certainly does prove to
possess physical fibre adequate to his ambition, if only because the
gap is narrowed by a plodding unimaginativeness at odds with his
supposed sensitivity.

The sexual ambivalences of the Crimsworth–Hunsden relationship dramatise an ideological struggle. To consolidate his social
progress requires of the Professor both a potentially rebellious
nonconformity and a prudently conservative moderation, as is
evident enough if he is contrasted with Edward on the one hand
and Hunsden on the other. From Edward's conservative standpoint,
his brother is a congenital misfit who throws up a secure job in the
name of freedom; from the viewpoint of Hunsden, the Whig re-
former and dashing Byronic sceptic, William is a pallid, meekly
cautious conservative. In fact Crimsworth, like Jane, is both spirited
*and* conventional; and like Jane too, although in a considerably
more conscious and ruthless way, he learns to turn his protective
self-possession to devastating advantage in his relentless power-
struggles with Mdlle Reuter and her unruly girl-pupils. He reaps
sadistic pleasure from the effects of his own impenetrability, enjoying the way Mdlle Reuter is stung by his coolness, quietly tearing
up a pupil's essay before her eyes. Crimsworth the victim becomes

Crimsworth the dominator;* like Jane, he turns his martyrdom to
fruitful profit in this world rather than the next.

Hunsden, too, is in his own way both radical and conservative,
a combination which evokes Crimsworth's mixed disapproval and
admiration. He is both gentleman and manufacturer, a 'tradesman' who is secretly proud of his 'ancient, if not high lineage'[12]
and is bidding to repair through trade the 'partially decayed
fortune of his house'.[13] He is a hard-headed anti-sentimentalist
but has a library well stocked with European literature and philosophy; he professes a meritocratic politics but despises Frances
Henri's humble status. He is both rebel and despot, and so a
'higher' expression of William's own ambivalently noncomformist
and autocratic temperament. And since his tyrannising over
Crimsworth assumes the form of goading him to rebel, Crimsworth
can know with him the pleasure of being both bullied and provoked, as he could not with his merely dictatorial kinsmen.
'. . . though [Hunsden] was neither like Crimsworth nor Lord
Tynedale, yet he was acrid, and, I suspected, overbearing in his
way; there was a tone of despotism in the urgency of the very
reproaches by which he aimed at goading the oppressed into rebellion against the oppressor.'[14] Hunsden, as an idealised Crimsworth, excels the aristocracy in sinew but beats the middle class
in culture; he is neither vulgar nor over-civilised, and since he is
thus something of a class-anomaly, William can pinpoint his
elusive style only as something literally foreign. 'In form and
feature he might be pronounced English, though even there one
caught a dash of something Gallic. . . .'[15] He prefigures a parallel
resolution of the foreign and familiar in the Anglo-Swiss Frances;
and the result in his case is an attractive equipoise of English
solidity and continental spirit:

> . . . he was not odd – no quiz – yet he resembled no one else I had
> ever seen before; his general bearing intimated complete,
> sovereign satisfaction with himself, yet, at times, an indescrib-
> able shade passed like an eclipse over his countenance, and
> seemed to me like the sign of a sudden and strong inward doubt

* It is of some interest in this context that Charlotte had been first
pupil, and then pupil-governess, at the Pensionnat Heger in Brussels; like
Crimsworth she knew the power-relationship from both ends.

of himself, his words and actions – an energetic discontent at his
life or his social position, his future prospects or his mental
attainments – I know not which; perhaps after all it might
only be a bilious caprice.[16]

Hunsden is neither too quirky nor too stolid; he is unique but not
odd, secure but not complacent, restless but not distraught. It is
not difficult to see the allure of this equipoise for a man like
Crimsworth, who finds in Hunsden a mirror-image of his own
covertly dissentient spirit but sees it enacted with all the stylish
authority of one secure in the worldly success he himself lacks.
Yet the relationship is not without its conflicts and ambiguities.
Crimsworth, who is both bourgeois and 'blood' aristocrat, finds
Hunsden (bourgeois and 'natural' aristocrat) both seductive and
repelling. He is fascinating in his flair, enterprise and independence, but unpleasant and rather dangerous in his sardonic Whig
free-thinking:

> 'What a nobleman you would have made, William Crimsworth!
> You are cut out for one; pity Fortune has baulked Nature! Look
> at the features, figure, even to the hands – distinction all over –
> ugly distinction! Now, if you'd only an estate and a mansion,
> and a park, and a title, how you could play the exclusive, main-
> tain the rights of your class, train your tenantry in habits of
> respect to the peerage, oppose at every step the advancing power
> of the people, support your rotten order, and be ready for its
> sake to wade knee-deep in churls' blood; as it is, you've no
> power; you can do nothing; you're wrecked and stranded on the
> shores of commerce; forced into collision with practical men,
> with whom you cannot cope, for *you'll never be a tradesman.*'[17]

Crimsworth is downtrodden but would make an efficient oppressor;
Hunsden is imperious but speaks up for the poor. William dismisses his radical sarcasm as mere prejudice, but it is not difficult
to imagine the Crimsworth we know at the end of the novel
stoutly maintaining his hard-won class-rights and cultivating
reverence for rank. To the extent that Hunsden is an *inverted*
mirror-image of William, he must clearly be combated. He
scandalises those aspects of Crimsworth which are externalised in

his dutiful wife Frances: her meek piety and Romantic patriotism
provide an essential foil to Hunsden's racy inconoclasm:

'England is your country?' asked Frances.
'Yes.'
'And you don't like it?'
I'd be sorry to like it! A little corrupt, venal, lord-and-king
cursed nation, full of mucky pride (as they say in —shire) and
helpless pauperism; rotten with abuses, worm-eaten with prejudices!' . . .
'I was not thinking of the wretchedness and vice in England;
I was thinking of the good side – of what is elevated in your
character as a nation. . . . I am English too; half the blood in
my veins is English; thus I have a right to a double power of
patriotism, possessing an interest in two noble, free, and fortunate counties.'[18]

The foreignness of both Frances and Hunsden appeals to William:
it detaches them from the English class-system (so that marrying
a Swiss lace-maker seems less ignominious than marrying an English one), and also lends them an agreeable touch of Romantic
mystery. But whereas Hunsden's un-Englishness is unpatriotic –
he is a 'universal patriot' whose country is the world – Frances's
serves paradoxically to intensify her bond with England. For English society to be defended against Hunsden by a native would be
dangerously chauvinist; to have an outsider speak up for it is
pleasantly consolidating.

Crimsworth's relation to Hunsden, then, is shot through with
contradictions. His bourgeois values ally themselves in one direction with Hunsden's middle-class radicalism, in opposition to the
venal society which has forced him into exile; but Crimsworth
clearly cannot afford to endorse Hunsden's politics to the point
where he would risk undermining the very social order into which
he has so laboriously climbed. Hunsden can evidently afford his
free-thinking, as William cannot. On the other hand, in so far
as Hunsden's bluff rationalism aligns him with the obnoxious
Edward, Frances is needed as a representative of alternative,
Romantic-conservative values, including a respect for 'blood'
aristocracy; but the two positions are saved from outright hostility
by the fact that Hunsden's personal energy and impeccable pedigree

render him impressive in Romantic-conservative eyes. For the progressive Whig capitalist, the traditional social order is merely obstructive and superannuated; for the traditional aristocrat turned prosperous non-commercial bourgeois, that order still has its value. The final relationship between Crimsworth and William, then, is one of antagonistic affection; their conflicts remain active but are gathered into pragmatic unity. On their return to England, William and Frances settle, significantly, next to Hunsden's estate; they end up as effective equals, although still within a formal inequality (Hunsden's house, for instance, is a good deal larger than the Professor's). Having made enough money to enfranchise his estate, Hunsden has abandoned manufacture; the Professor has also made his fortune, given up work, and will now seal the alliance between aristocracy and bourgeoisie for the next generation by sending his son to Eton. Frances and Hunsden, meanwhile, continue their political wrangling, but they can afford to; with all the material issues successfully resolved, nothing is now at stake but a difference of conversational viewpoint.

If Crimsworth draws stimulus from his self-indulgent conflict with Hunsden, he takes even greater delight in playing cat and mouse with Mdlle Reuter. Here, indeed, he has the definite edge: he watches with ironic interest as she probes for his weak point, 'some chink, some niche, where she could put in her little firm foot and stand upon [his] neck – mistress of [his] nature'.[19] He treats her as Jane treats Rochester, only with more nakedly sadistic malice: 'I enjoyed the game much, and did not hasten its conclusion; sometimes I gave her hopes, beginning a sentence rather weakly, when her shrewd eye would light up – she thought she had me; having led her a little way, I delighted to turn round and finish with hard, sound sense, whereat her countenance would fall.'[20] Baffling Mdlle Reuter by his impervious blandness becomes the Professor's most absorbing pastime; he has perfected the technique while working for Edward, who soon 'tired of wasting his ammunition on a statue',[21] and now presents himself to Mddle Reuter as 'a smooth bare precipice, which offered neither jutting stone nor tree-root, nor tuft of grass to aid the climber'.[22] Whereas in *Villette* Lucy Snowe is suspicious of John Bretton's over-sanguine reaction to the unveiling of Ginevra Fanshawe's real character, sensing in this an absence of true passion, Crimsworth prides himself on not being piqued by the recognition that Mdlle Reuter is merely a flirt. 'That sting must have gone too deep for any consolations of philosophy to be available in curing its smart? Not at all. . . . Reason was my physician; she began by proving that the prize I had missed was of little value: she admitted that, physically, Zoraïde might have suited me, but affirmed that our souls were not in harmony, and that discord must have resulted from the union of her mind with mine.'[23] *Villette* is a more authentic because more disturbed book than *The Professor*; Crimsworth is a utopian male version of Lucy, shorn for the most part of her suffering and self-doubt. Whereas Lucy Snowe, after an initial parade of unconvincing self-composure, grows more credibly distraught as the novel progresses, the Professor grows more unpleasantly invulnerable.

This is particularly obvious in his relationship with Frances. As an amalgam of English and European, working-girl and gentle-woman, pupil and teacher, child and adult, Frances represents precisely that blend of the docile and socially desirable which would attract Crimsworth. She may teach lace-mending – 'A dull, stupid occupation', William briskly informs her – but her voice is 'a voice of Albion; the accent was pure and silvery; it only wanted firmness, and assurance, to be the counter-part of what any well educated young lady in Essex or Middlesex might have enounced'.[24] By the grace of Crimsworth, Frances is finally transformed into such a genteel young Englishwoman, although she clearly cannot be allowed too much firmness and assurance if his connubial authority is to be preserved. The Professor revels self-indulgently in his power over her: he knows that 'Servility creates despotism',[25] and reflects that 'Human beings . . . seldom deny themselves the pleasure of exercising a power which they are conscious of possessing, even though the power consist only in a capacity to make others wretched'.[26] He certainly experiences such dominance in his general dealings with foreigners: he demurs at M. Pelet's racist attitude to the Flemish ('I could not see why their being aboriginals of the flat, dull soil should serve as a pretext for treating them with perpetual severity and contempt'[27]) but holds precisely the same view of his Belgian students, whom he compares obliquely to clamorous swine.

Dominated by the dashing Hunsden, Crimsworth compensates

by bullying Frances, whose lamb-like devotion to him he smugly savours. His descriptions of her to Hunsden are vulgarly reifying: she is his 'little wild strawberry', a 'narrative' full of 'sweet variety and thrilling excitement.'[28] Yet Frances herself is a 'curious mixture of tractability and firmness';[29] she continues to call him 'Monsieur' after their marriage, but also has a 'certain proud impatience' which makes her chafe against his tutorial help, and she can be as sour as Crimsworth with her pupils:

> I heard her say, suddenly and sharply, addressing one of the eldest and most turbulent of the lot,
> 'Amélie Müllenberg, ask me no question, and request of me no assistance, for a week to come; during that space of time I will neither speak to you nor help you'.[30]

It is important that William overhears this, since it displays a spirit in Frances which allows him to repress her with an easy conscience. He can persuade himself not only that she has the resources to withstand his censoriousness but that it actually does her good:

> The reproofs suited her the best of all: while I scolded she would chip away with her pen-knife at a pencil or a pen; fidgeting a little, pouting a little, defending herself by monosyllables, and when I deprived her of the pen or pencil, fearing it would be all cut away, and when I interdicted even the monosyllabic defence, for the purpose of working up the subdued excitement a little higher, she would at last raise her eyes and give me a certain glance, sweetened with gaiety, and pointed with defiance, which, to speak truth, thrilled me as nothing had ever done, and made me, in a fashion (though happily she did not know it), her subject, if not her slave.[31]

With Frances, Crimsworth can erotically sample the simultaneous enthralments of mastery and submission, in a transparently sado-masochistic relationship.

He is not always, however, quite as candid as in that last quotation. Elsewhere he rationalises his perverse dealings with Frances as the necessary assumption of a role, prickly on the outside but tender within:

Constancy of attention – a kindness as mute as watchful, always standing by her, cloaked in the rough garb of austerity, and making its real nature known only by a rare glance of interest, or a cordial and gentle word; real respect masked with seeming imperiousness, directing, urging her actions yet helping her too, and that with devoted care: these were the means I used, for these means best suited Frances' feelings, as susceptible as deep vibrating – her nature, at once proud and shy.[82]

This recalls Paul Emmanuel in *Villette*; but Crimsworth is a less convincing rough diamond than Paul. We have Lucy's word for Paul's bluffly concealed kindness, whereas we have only Crimsworth's word for his own; and what we actually see of his behaviour hardly bears it out. The novelist of *Villette* divides her imaginative sympathies between Paul and Lucy, whereas William, as both lonely expatriate and irascible schoolmaster, is effectively a conflation of the two. The point of that conflation is to endow the victim from the outset with qualities of toughness and command, and so to idealise his vulnerability almost out of existence. It is then left to Frances to play the role of the suffering Lucy; but since she is seen always from Crimsworth's viewpoint, and so externally, those tones of anxiety remain firmly subdued.

Charlotte wrote in her Preface to *The Professor* that her hero was intended to 'work his way through life as I have seen real living men work theirs – that he should never get a shilling he had not earned – that no sudden turns should lift him in a moment to wealth and high station; that whatsoever small competency he might gain should be won by the sweat of his brow'.[83] The novel on the whole bears out this meritocratic myth, but a significant qualification must be made. It is true that Crimsworth scorns aristocratic patronage and prospers by his own initiative; but one reason why he can do so is because he is after all an aristocrat by birth, furnished with privileged accomplishments which he can put to profitable use. In one sense he defeats the nobility at their own despicable game, achieving wealth and leisure without enduring the indignities of paternalism; but he can do this because in qualities of character he is still an integral part of that game. It is just that he, unlike traditional aristocrats such as Tynedale, treats those 'innate' or acquired traits as social commodities, investing them where he can reap most return.* At one level, *The Professor* could be said to be an inversion of *Jane Eyre*: whereas that novel showed a bourgeoise elevated to the gentry, this one shows an aristocrat transformed into a bourgeois. Yet the difference, for all the striking imaginative distance between the two works, is purely superficial, a question of two variations of a single categorical structure.† The point about both Jane and Crimsworth is that they are socially 'impure' – exiles, hybrids, outcasts, ambiguous figures trapped at a point of tension between alternative classes and competing ideologies. As such, they are 'typical' characters in a Lukácsian sense of the term – figures whose very ambivalence calls into play a whole pattern of contending historical forces.[84] It is precisely because William Crimsworth is directly assimilable to no one of these forces – he is neither industrial capitalist nor landed aristocrat, rebellious radical nor despotic reactionary – that he focuses most acutely their significant interplay. He is, to adopt a metaphor of Brecht's, the stage on which those historical contradictions work themselves out; like Jane Eyre, he is at once 'insider' and 'outsider', and so encompasses in his own person a whole spectrum of social conflicts. The point of the narrative, then, is to chart the process by which those conflicts press through to a precarious resolution: to trace the tentative rapprochement between Whig inconoclasm and Tory piety, bourgeois drive and leisured domesticity, radical protest and conservative patriotism.

* A fact symbolised in a minor way by the incident in which Crimsworth saves the son of the wealthy Vandenhuten from drowning, and subsequently profits financially from Vandenhuten's gratitude. Crimsworth directly attributes the efficiency of the rescue to a boyhood at Eton: 'My coat and waistcoat were off in an instant; I had not been brought up at Eton and bathed and swam there for ten years for nothing; it was a natural and easy act for me to leap to the rescue.' The Vandenhuten incident is not, perhaps, a 'sudden turn' in Crimsworth's fortunes; but it is through Vandenhuten's patronage that he attains the teaching post which sets him on the path to prosperity, and to that extent there seems a dissonance between what the novel shows and what the Preface claims for it.

† Thus, whether Jane is actually bourgeois or 'gentry' in origin remains obscure; and Crimsworth's 'aristocratic' background is similarly mixed.

# 3 Shirley

*Shirley* was published in 1849, one year after the defeat of Chartism; and yet, though the novel is much preoccupied with class-conflict, it is backdated to the Luddite events of 1812. It is worth enquiring why this should be so. The West Riding of the 1840s was an intensive focus of Chartist agitation: Leeds was second only to Manchester as a centre of radical insurgency, and produced the most influential of all Chartist organs, the *Northern Star*. During the Plug strikes of 1842 some six thousand workers brought mills in the villages around Leeds to a standstill; five years later, severe economic depression, high unemployment and soaring food-prices generated a significant Chartist revival. In 1848 West Riding workers were arming and drilling; two thousand of them clashed in that year at Bradford with an equivalent number of soldiers and police.[1] Yet *Shirley* chooses to ignore contemporary conditions, imaginatively translating them to an earlier phase of the Yorkshire class-struggle, negotiating its feelings in relation to the past rather than the present.

Backdating of this kind is in any case characteristic of Charlotte's fiction. The autobiographical material drawn on by the other three novels is distanced to display the fleshed and rounded shape of an achieved career, a life which labours through (with the ambiguous exception of *Villette*) to a good end. In so far as Charlotte's novels are success-stories, such distancing is essential; and when *Shirley* was written the contemporary class-struggle was still too fraught and precarious an issue to render it an ideal context for such an assured outcome. Even so, there can be no doubt that Chartism is the unspoken subject of *Shirley*. In common with most members of her class, Charlotte Brontë feared revolution in 1848; writing to a friend in March of that year,

she expressed her belief that 'convulsive revolutions put back the
world in all that is good, check civilisation, bring the dregs of
society to its surface. . . . That England may be spared the spasms,
cramps, and frenzy-fits now contorting the Continent and threatening Ireland, I earnestly pray!'² Less than a month later, after the
final defeat of the Charter, she confided to another correspondent
her opinion that the Chartists 'should not indeed be neglected, nor
the existence of their sufferings ignored. It would now be the right
time, when an ill-advised movement has been judiciously repressed, to examine carefully into their causes of complaint, and
make such concessions as justice and humanity dictate. If Govern-
ment would act so, how much good might be done by the removal
of ill-feeling and the substitution of mutual kindliness in its
place!'³ It is a familiar enough case: smash the enemy and then
bend a paternalist ear from a position of strength.

Yet that curious blend of Gaskellian liberalism and Welling-
tonian reaction says much about the politics of *Shirley*. *Shirley*
deals with historical events which closely concern the relations
between Tory squirearchy and Whig manufacturers in the West
Riding of the time. The central dramatic incident of the novel –
the Luddite attack on Robert Moore's mill – re-creates the assault
in 1812 on William Cartwright's mill at Liversedge in the Spen
Valley; and Cartwright's ruthless repulsion of the Luddites sig-
nalled, in Edward Thompson's words, 'a profound emotional reconciliation between the large mill-owners and the authorities'⁴ at a
time when squire and mill-owner were bitterly hostile to one
another over the war and the Orders in Council. The Liversedge
assault was part of the Brontë sisters' childhood mythology: they
heard lurid tales of it from their headmistress, Miss Wooler,
whose school at Roe Head was not far from the Cartwright
factory; and Patrick Brontë, who took a characteristically authoritarian line about Luddism, had to carry about a loaded pistol to
protect himself from local mill-workers.⁵ The main ideological
thrust of *Shirley* is to re-create and celebrate that class-con-
solidation between squire and mill-owner, achieved as it was by
the catalyst of working-class militancy; and it is for this reason
that the novel is at once backdated to Luddism and relevant to its
own time. What interests Charlotte about Luddism is hardly at all
the nature of working-class protest but its effect on the complex

alignment of interests within the ruling class; and that historical closing of ranks is obviously relevant to the problem of how to confront Chartism. At the end of *Shirley*, Robert Moore, having 'judiciously repressed' Luddite militancy, is faced as an employer with the dictates of 'justice and humanity'; and we have little doubt that, given the good offices of Caroline Helstone, he will encounter those demands successfully. The Luddite events, then, relate as both promise and warning to the moment of Chartism; *Shirley* selects a period of class-conflict which is known, retrospectively, to have had a 'good' outcome, and demonstrates how that resolution may be re-achieved in the turbulent conditions of contemporary England.

The novel's major political thrust, then, is to re-create a moment of historical rapprochement between warring sectors of the ruling class – a rapprochement which, need one say, is of the utmost relevance to the bitter class-struggles of the 1840s.* *Shirley* belongs to that contemporary structure of consciousness, evident enough in Carlyle and Young England, which deflects the demands of the workers by shifting attention to the quality of their rulers. The upshot of such a shift is to seal the given structure of class-relations while anxiously refurbishing its moral texture. Yet here *Shirley* has an edge over Carlyle and Disraeli: whereas they plunge into an improbable organic past, excavating it for reinhabitation, *Shirley* moves a mere forty years back into history, but in doing so reopens and relives a crucial moment in the genesis of the present. If the ruling class was able to unite in the face of Luddism, then, confronted with the Chartist threat, it can do so once again.

To say that the raid on Robert Moore's mill is the 'central dramatic incident' of *Shirley* needs immediate qualification. It would be truer to say that the event is at once structurally central and curiously empty – empty because the major protagonist, the working class, is distinguished primarily by its absence. It is instructive to examine how the affair is actually presented. It is seen

* The two historical phases, Luddism and Chartism, were indeed not so separate: J. F. C. Harrison points out (*op. cit.*) how the 'outer shape' of West Riding Chartism was determined by the region's previous history of radicalism. His analysis of the divisions which Chartism created within the ruling class also has a bearing on the subject-matter of *Shirley*.

from the vantage-point of Caroline and Shirley; but 'seen' is not
quite the word. Watching from the Rectory window, the girls
hear first the 'dull tramp of marching feet. . . . It was not the
tread of two, nor of a dozen, nor of a score of men; it was the
tread of hundreds.'⁶ They can, however, see nothing: 'the high
shrubs of the garden formed a leafy screen between them and the
road'.⁷ Dashing to the mill, their perception of the event remains
purely auditory:

> A crash – smash – shiver – stopped their whispers. A simultane-
> ously-hurled volley of stones had saluted the broad front of the
> mill, with all its windows; and now every pane of every lattice
> lay in shattered and pounded fragments. A yell followed this
> demonstration – a rioters' yell – a North-of-England – a York-
> shire – a West-Riding – a West-Riding-clothing-district of York-
> shire rioters' yell. You never heard that sound, perhaps, reader?
> So much the better for your ears – perhaps for your heart;
> since, if it rends the air in hate to yourself, or to the men or
> principles you approve, the interests to which you wish well,
> Wrath wakens to the cry of Hate: the Lion shakes his mane,
> and rises to the howl of the Hyena: Caste stands up, ireful,
> against Caste; and the indignant, wronged spirit of the Middle
> Rank bears down in zeal and scorn on the famished and furious
> mass of the Operative Class. It is difficult to be tolerant –
> difficult to be just – in such moments.⁸

The distance of this from any detailed realisation, obvious enough
in the abstraction of action to sound, emerges as much in the
dramatic slackness which allows the author to turn and button-
hole the reader at the very peak of crisis as it does in the straying,
facetious self-indulgence of those fanciful compound epithets.
Action is displaced into portentously inflated allegory – an allegory
which incites us to indulge the very emotions it formally censors.
Still nothing can actually be seen: 'What was going on now? It
seemed difficult, in the darkness, to distinguish, but something
terrible, a still-renewing tumult, was obvious; fierce attacks, desperate repulses; the mill-yard, the mill itself, was full of battle-
movement: there was scarcely any cessation now of the discharge
of firearms; and there was struggling, rushing, trampling, and
shouting between.'⁹ It is left to the hectic, fragmentary syntax to

retrieve a faint sense of the excitement blankly dispelled by the perfunctory notations of the prose. *Seeing* is possible only when the incident is over: the sun rises to reveal the debris of the battle, and since the agents of the affray have now withdrawn, they can be characterised only by a return to the depersonalising allegorical mode: 'Discord, broken loose in the night from control, had beaten the ground with his stamping hoofs, and left it waste and pulverized.'[10] At the point of its most significant presence in the novel, the working class is wholly invisible.

It is therefore not surprising to find that, when the workers do put in a collective appearance in the novel in the confrontation between their spokesman Moses Barraclough and Robert Moore, the style of presentation is that of caricature:

> Twelve men waited in the yard, some in their shirt-sleeves, some in blue aprons: two figures conspicuously in the van of the party. One, a little dapper strutting man, with a turned-up nose; the other, a broad-shouldered fellow, distinguished no less by his demure face and cat-like, trustless eyes, than by a wooden leg and stout crutch: there was a kind of leer about his lips, he seemed laughing in his sleeve at some person or thing, his whole air was anything but that of a true man.[11]*

Even Barraclough's leg is denied authenticity. His counterpart in the novel is William Farren, a model of decency and good manners who is present largely to provide Shirley and Caroline with an object of patronage; and the novel's attitude to the working class wavers accordingly between panicky contempt and paternalist condescension. The workers' plight is regretted, but nothing can be done: it is sad that those thrown out of work by technological innovation are left to suffer, but they are 'perhaps inevitably left:

---

* Charlotte's lurid travesty of the Luddites may be placed beside Eric Hobsbawm's comments in *Labouring Men* that Luddism, far from being some merely mindless wrecking, was a calculated attempt to use attacks on machines to coerce employers into granting concessions in wages and working conditions. In many cases there was no question of any hostility to the machine as such; wrecking was simply a technique of trade unionism during the early phases of the industrial revolution. Even where there was hostility to the machine as such, it was shared by a great mass of public opinion, including that of many employers.

it would not do to stop the progress of invention, to damage
science by discouraging its improvements. . . .'[12]

If the workers of *Shirley* are for the most part freaks or dis-
embodied roars, this is partly because the novel, as I have suggested,
is in no sense directly concerned with them. It is preoccupied with
certain structural contradictions within the ruling class itself; and
it is here that the character of Shirley assumes importance. Shirley
is a landowner, but half her income comes from owning a mill;
and even though her attitude to the mill is callowly aesthetic (she
is 'tickled with an agreeable complacency'[13]* when she thinks of it),
she is adamant that trade is to be respected, and determined to
defend her property like a tigress. 'If once the poor gather and rise
in the form of a mob', she tells Caroline Helstone, 'I shall turn
against them as an aristocrat.'[15] The novel registers a few feeble
liberal protests against this position: Caroline ventures to point
out the injustice of including all working people under the term
'mob', and elsewhere Shirley, with no sense of inconsistency and
conveniently enough for herself in the circumstances, can denounce
all crying-up of one class against another. But her 'spirited' attitude
is in general endorsed, not least because it has behind it the
weight of her ancient Yorkshire lineage, with its traditions of
paternalist care for the poor. Indeed, because she is a conservative paternalist, Shirley's position can accommodate a fair amount
of reformism: she objects to the Church's insolence to the poor and
servility to the rich, and believes it to be 'in the utmost need of
reformation'.[16] In this sense she differs from Robert Moore, whose
neglect of philanthropy as a manufacturer is implicitly connected
with his ill-luck in not having been born a Yorkshireman. But
although Moore is critically measured against the robust traditions of Yorkshire paternalism, it is, significantly, Shirley herself
who bails him out financially and leaps to the defence of his personal callousness. He is, she points out, a man who entered the
district poor and friendless, with nothing but his own energies to
back him; and it is unfair to upbraid him for not having been able
to 'popularise his naturally grave, quiet manners, all at once'.[17]
(Moore's original, Cartwright, who defended his property with

---

* This seems a common phenomenon of the period. Some landowners'
diaries and letters show a taste for viewing mills, mines and furnaces as
pronounced as that for a classical prospect.[14]

soldiers, spiked barricades and a tub of vitriol, and is reputed to have refused injured Luddites water or a doctor unless they turned informer, seems less easily excusable on the grounds of shyness.[18]) It is, in other words, the representative of the gentry who comes to the moral and material rescue of the bourgeois manufacturer; and Moore is in any case defended by the novel by a use of the 'split self' image which suggests that a sensitive dreamer lurks behind his 'hard dog' exterior.

As a hybrid of progressive capitalist and traditional landowner, then, Shirley provides an important defence of trade; unlike the die-hard Tory Helstone, who finds 'the cloth – the greasy wool – the polluting dyeing vats'[19] distasteful, she regards the woollen industry as something to be 'thoroughly respected' and admires Moore as a Carlylean captain of industry ('Prince is on his brow, and ruler in his bearing'[20]). But her charismatic presence in the novel is also needed to defend Romantic conservatism against bourgeois rationalism. Although she tells Helstone that half her income comes from the mill, she later adjusts that proportion to rather less than half, confesses 'rather a leaning to the agricultural interest',[21] and gently chides industrialists for their greed. There are manufacturing families in the district boasting twice Shirley's income, but 'the Keeldars, by virtue of their antiquity, and their distinction of lords of the manor, took the precedence of all'.[22] She is, for instance, notably hard on the radical capitalist Yorke, whose doctrinaire Whiggism she sees as unfitting him for true reform; and the novel itself underscores this judgement by its stern emphasis on Yorke's lack of 'veneration'. Shirley, in other words, stands to Yorke as Frances Crimsworth stands to Hunsden: both radicals are admired for their verve and fighting Yorkshire blood (qualities on which *Shirley* in particular places tediously chauvinistic stress), but their brash lack of reverence counts heavily against them. Yorke has the advantage of being 'thoroughly English, not a Norman line anywhere';[23] his pith, sagacity and intelligence are inseparable from an inelegant Northern harshness, but so also are the scorn and sarcasm which lead him to dismiss kings, nobles and priests as so much rubbish. He is a kindly paternalist employer who, like Hunsden, espouses liberty and equality, but betrays an innate haughtiness and instinctive authoritarianism.

Yorke then, like Hunsden, is an amalgam of radical bourgeois and natural aristocrat – rough, racy but discreetly cultured, able when he likes to display the manners of a 'finished gentleman of the old school'.[24] To this extent he has something of Hunsden's perverse appeal; but it is clear too that he receives markedly rougher treatment at the novel's hands than Hunsden does. There are two reasons for this. One is that *Shirley* is a more intensively ideological work than *The Professor*: given its background of social crisis, it needs urgently to protect conservative pieties against a Whiggism more immediately subversive of the social fabric than Hunsden's was. The other reason is that if Yorke combines libertarian revolt with proud autocracy, Shirley trumps that position by doing the same more desirably. 'More desirably' means, primarily, both more romantically and more conservatively: Shirley has the imagination which Yorke lacks, but she also blends revolt and reverence in a way which tips the balance decisively on the side of the *status quo*. This must not, of course, be too obvious if the image of Shirley as Romantic radical is to be maintained; and the novel has occasionally to resort to some devious stratagems to ensure that image's credibility. Shirley's impassioned attack on Yorke's generous defence of the Luddites is a case in point. Her arguments are strikingly shabby: she excuses Moore (as we have seen) on the grounds of his foreignness, romanticises his lonely stand against 'two hundred' without reference to the substantial rights of the situation, suggests that Yorke himself would be less radical if he were in power or under pressure, and diverts the political debate to *ad hominem* invective. Her most remarkable achievement, however, is to cast a reactionary case into terms which make it appear even more radical than Yorke's:

> I wonder people cannot judge more fairly of each other and themselves. When I hear Messrs Malone and Donne chatter about the authority of the Church, and dignity and claims of the priesthood, the deference due to them as clergymen; when I hear the outbreaks of their small spite against Dissenters . . . I recall your senseless sarcasms on the 'fat bishops', the 'pampered parsons', 'old mother church', etc. I remember your strictures on all who differ from you, your sweeping condemnation of classes and individuals, without the slightest allowance made

for circumstances or temptations; and then, Mr Yorke, doubt
clutches my inmost heart as to whether men exist clement,
reasonable, and just enough to be intrusted with the task of
reform. I don't believe *you* are of the number.'[25]

The argument, beneath its covering moral intensity, is subtly oppor-
tunistic. *Shirley* succeeds adroitly in fusing a radical assault on the
clergy with a conservative defence of them against Yorke's very
similar criticisms, maintaining her own orthodoxy while deftly
stealing Yorke's radical clothes. A progressive rejection of ecclesiastical bigotry merges into an assault on Yorke's narrow-minded-
ness, so that Yorke and the clerics seem suddenly equated, with
Shirley herself assuming the alternative liberal posture of 'fairness'
and 'justice'. Fairness, however, cuts both ways: it is claimed as a
reformist virtue, but since it means making humane allowance
for 'circumstances and temptations', it also signifies a tolerant
acceptance of the *status quo*. The emptiness of Shirley's 'liberal'
stance is obvious enough in her fierce denunciation of Yorke's
politics as despicable partisanship rather than just impartiality.
To speak up for Luddites is prejudice, to defend the employers
nobly disinterested.

    Shirley's 'radicalism', in fact, is less a matter of doctrine than
of style; as with Felix Holt, flashing eyes and a forceful physical
presence go some way towards coating a conservative case with a
glossy layer of radicalism. Her radicalism is in fact the spirited
individualism of the aristocrat, and so is politically ambiguous: it is
equally 'spirited' to help the poor or shoot them down, and
Shirley is prepared to do both. Indeed, the novel is clear that if
you don't do one you may be forced to do the other: Shirley's
charity, she tells Caroline, is aimed at allaying the poor's suffering
and so assuaging their potentially dangerous class-hatred. She is,
nevertheless, concerned to see something better than mere 'deference from acquaintance, and homage from the poor';[26] she is
moderately blasé about the trappings of social rank, and Caroline
feels in her society 'a safe sense of equality . . . never known in
that of the ordinary Briarfield and Whinbury gentry'.[27] In this
sense she is socially progressive, in contrast with Caroline's
improbably long-lost mother Mrs Pryor, to whom it is left to
deliver the most explicit formulation of the reverence which Yorke

blasphemously lacks. 'Implicit submission to authorities, scrupu-
lous deference to our betters (under which term I, of course,
include the higher classes of society) are, in my opinion, indis-
pensable to the wellbeing of every community'.[28] Mrs Pryor's
Toryism is affectionately satirised – 'of all the high and rigid
Tories', Shirley remarks, 'she is queen'[29] – but she is, after all,
Caroline's mother and Shirley's ex-governess, and so carries a
moral weight which is not to be easily discounted.

Commerce, in the novel's view, represents a genuine threat to
Mrs Pryor's vision of heirarchical harmony. The mercantile classes,
Charlotte Brontë comments, deny chivalrous feeling, disinterestedness and pride of honour in their narrowly unpatriotic scramble
for gain:

> All men, taken singly, are more or less selfish; and taken in
> bodies they are intensely so. The British merchant is no excep-
> tion to this rule: the mercantile classes illustrate it strikingly.
> These classes certainly think too exclusively of making money;
> they are too oblivious of every national consideration but that
> of extending England's (*i.e.* their own) commerce. . . . A land
> ruled by them alone would too often make ignominious sub-
> mission – not at all from the motives Christ teaches, but rather
> from those Mammon instills. . . .
>
> Long may it be ere England really becomes a nation of shop-
> keepers![30]

Capitalism denies, in fact, the aristocratic, Romantic-conservative
values; and part of the novel's point is to validate those neglected
virtues without adopting too obviously the bigoted 'Church-and-
King' posture of Helstone, Caroline's military-parson guardian.
This is simple enough, given the novel's structure, since between
the formalist Helstone and the free-thinking Yorke stands Shirley,
paradigm of the desired union between Romanticism and reform,
gentry and capitalist, order and progress. By the end of the novel,
indeed, that union is literal as well as symbolic: Moore, having
recovered his fortunes by the repeal of the Orders in Council, and
having been suitably humanised as an employer by Caroline's
influence, will add to the income of Shirley (who has married his
brother Louis), double the value of her mill-property and build

cottages which Shirley will then let to his own workmen. The bond between squire and mill-owner is indissolubly sealed.*

One reason why it can be sealed, however, is because the Moore brothers are no common bourgeois. Their family has a respectable two-centuries-old tradition of trade, so that although the collapse of its fortunes means that Robert has had to begin in England from scratch, this goes to underline his heroic initiative rather than reveal him as vulgarly *nouveau riche*. That initiative is a personal attribute which differentiates him from those traditionalist gentlemen like Helstone who think only in terms of rank; but since it is also the product of a long genetic inheritance, it suggests the workings of some vaguely patrician 'blood'. This particular ambiguity – the sense that Moore is at once isolated individualist and spiritually of the gentry – is reflected in the crucial fact of his foreignness. In one way that foreignness serves to emphasise his individualism: he is an alien in England, indifferent to patriotism and local custom, relying purely on his own abilities as Crimsworth did in Europe. As the novel's primary type of industrial capitalism Moore is suitably stateless, owing allegiance to profit rather than social piety. Yet his foreignness is also an engaging Romantic trait: it allies him obscurely to race and blood, and to that extent links him indirectly with traditional Yorkshire, rather as Hunsden's Yorkshire blood suggested conversely a vaguely Gallic flavour. Yorke, who claims that Moore's blood is as pure as Shirley's, recognises the affinity; and in any case Moore's father was a Yorkshireman. In so far as his indifference to Yorkshire paternalism reflects his ruthlessness as an employer, he serves to show up the superiority of Shirley's native traditions; but the fact of being foreign is also exploited to excuse his brutality. In one sense the novel's recurrent appeal to 'blood' works against the rootless Moore; but since his pedigree, though foreign, is distinguished, 'blood' provides a transcultural tie between himself and the West Riding gentry. He belongs to that world sufficiently to consort with Shirley on equal terms, but is enough of an *émigré* to exude an intriguing air of continental mystery. As an

* Materially, that is: the novel actually ends on a muted note of *ideological* dissonance between Romantic traditionalism and bourgeois progress, centred on Caroline's distaste for Moore's plans to destroy the natural scenery of Briarfield valley by industrialisation.

c

employer he is a good deal tougher than Yorke, but his 'Gallic'
saturnine sensitivity gives him a personal edge over the native
capitalist.

It is worth noting that, though a preoccupation with race and
blood runs throughout Charlotte's fiction, it is probably stronger
in *Shirley* than elsewhere – stronger, that is to say, in the novel
which deals most directly with class-struggle. By means of this
racial ideology, a partial, purely factitious resolution of class-
conflict can be magically effected. Yorkshire spirit transcends
class-divisions: the 'majority of the lads and lasses of the West
Riding are gentlemen and ladies, every inch of them',[31] so that,
confronted with impudent Cockneys, effete aristocrats or doltish
Irish clerics, the unifying bonds between Yorkshire gentleman and
mill-worker assume deeper significance than that which divides
them. (Shirley and William Farren, for example, are akin in their
Yorkshire pride.) As in *Jane Eyre*, this metaphorical (indeed
mystical) meaning of gentility cuts partly across its concrete social
sense; Shirley rejects the suit of Sir Philip Nunneley because, noble-
man though he is, he is spiritually unworthy of her, and marries
instead into the middle class. Yet, again as in *Jane Eyre*, metaphorical gentility is a half-way house between equality and hierarchy: Louis Moore is sufficiently well-bred to prove a socially
acceptable husband for Shirley, who is not after all of the highest
aristocratic rank and cannot, she is told, hope to marry into the
peerage. The appeal to blood works against the inflexible class-
prejudice of a Helstone, who cannot see how Robert Moore can be
a true gentleman; but Shirley's liberalising of Helstone's conservative categories ironically means defending the man who is the
major cause of social division.

If Romantic conservatism and bourgeois realism conclude an
alliance in the novel's main action, the conflict between them
is most vividly focused in the figure of Caroline Helstone. Caroline is the typical Charlotte heroine, of whom Shirley is a heavily
idealised version; and I shall say more in a later chapter about
the structural significance of this splitting of roles. It is enough
to say here that Caroline suffers an acute crisis of identity from
which Shirley is protected by virtue of her social privilege. Whereas the world is pliant to Shirley's assured touch, Romantic impulse
and material reality meet for Caroline only in deadlock:

You held out your hand for an egg, and fate put into it a scorpion. Show no consternation; close your fingers firmly upon the
gift; let it sting through your palm. Never mind: in time, after
your hand and arm have swelled and quivered long with torture,
the squeezed scorpion will die, and you will have learnt the
great lesson how to endure without a sob. . . . Nature . . . is an
excellent friend in such cases; sealing the lips, interdicting
utterance, commanding a placid dissimulation. . . .[32]

It is a conflict between private agony and bland public mask
common in Charlotte's fiction – an awareness of one's pulsating
life negated to dull anonymity by an indifferent society. Ironically,
Caroline's only release from torment would be into the very role
which sharpens the contradiction most, that of governess. (Her
mother tells her how her own life as a governess was 'sedentary,
solitary, constrained, joyless, toilsome'.[33]) For Caroline as for
Jane, becoming a governess is ambivalently escape and imprison-
ment, free choice and fatality: 'But one project could she frame
whose execution seemed likely to bring her a hope of relief; it was
to take a situation to be a governess – she could do nothing else.'[34]
Driven into solitary brooding by her unrequited love for Moore,
Caroline is the novel's vulnerable point, the 'fault' through
which feelings otherwise repressed (Moore) or confidently achieved
(Shirley) burst into spontaneous exposure. She represents that
troubled, restlessly subjective dimension which the novel's optimis-
tic politics expel; and as such she embodies one aspect of authorial
consciousness as Shirley reveals another, playing – to adopt an
excessively imprecise analogy – Lucy Snowe to Shirley's admirably
self-sufficient Paul Emmanuel.
      Caroline, however, is not to be abandoned to servitude; in-
stead, she marries Robert Moore. Their relationship, given Moore's
imperiousness, is of course unequal, but like Jane's union with
Rochester it involves a civilising influence: she promises Robert
that she 'will take faithful care of him',[35] which implies a certain
tactful control as well as obedient service. A considerably more
pronounced dialectic of power and submissiveness, however, is at
work in the strongly sado-masochistic relationship between Shirley
and Louis Moore. Shirley is stoutly independent and believes in
sexual equality; and, like Blanche Ingram, her style of sexual

self-assertion is to usurp the role of male power. She is a masculine woman holding 'a man's position' as landowner; indeed, 'Shirley' is the male family name her parents intended to give to a son. The novel's feminism thus divides between Caroline's moving but timidly gradualist pleas for greater social opportunities, and the maundering rhetoric of Shirley's embarrassing feminist mysticism: 'The first woman's breast that heaved with life on this world yielded the daring which could contend with Omnipotence. . . . The first woman was heaven-born: vast was the heart whence gushed the well-spring of the blood of nations. . . .'[36] Shirley is a superior 'male' version of Caroline, whom she physically resembles; and she thus becomes for Caroline an ideal self-image to be revered, in a latently sexual relationship. Despite her claims to sexual independence, however, Shirley yearns to be sexually mastered, and rejects Sir Philip Nunneley because he would never sufficiently command her. 'I will accept no hand which cannot hold me in check. . . . Did I not say I prefer a *master*? . . . A man whose appro-bation can reward – whose displeasure punish me.'[37] Louis Moore, despite his reserved exterior, turns out to be a fit candidate for the role:

> 'My wife, if I ever marry, must stir my great frame with a sting now and then. . . . I was not made so enduring to be mated with a lamb: I should find more congenial responsibility in the charge of a young lioness or leopardess . . . my patience would exult in stilling the flutterings and training the energies of the restless merlin. In managing the wild instincts of the scarce manageable 'bête fauve', my powers would revel.'[38]

The four-cornered relationship between Shirley, Caroline, Robert and Louis is significantly complicated. Shirley and Caroline are alike, and so are Robert and Louis; Shirley is more successful than Caroline and Robert more successful than Louis, but in each case the more and less successful characters marry. The 'right' marriage relations would seem to be Shirley–Robert and Caroline–Louis; but these relations are inverted, and it is important to under-stand why. Shirley provides Caroline with a kind of sexual surro-gate for Robert: she is introduced into the novel when Caroline is in the throes of frustrated passion, in order to sublimate and displace the sexual feelings which Moore fails to reciprocate. She

is both a Romantic idealisation of Caroline herself and attractively
'other'; and this, indeed, is an ambiguity inherent in all hero-
worship, where the venerator wants and does not want to be the
venerated, yearns to unite with the hero while cherishing the
differentiating distance between them. The novel solves this
ambiguity by having Shirley marry Louis, who, as a spiritually
cultivated, apparently docile subordinate, is a kind of male type
of Caroline. Through the *persona* of Louis, then, Caroline is vicari-
ously united with her heroine; and since she also marries Robert,
who seemed more predictably Shirley's husband, Caroline becomes
Shirley in this sense too.

Becoming Shirley in this second sense, however, involves ousting
her: Caroline gets Robert and Shirley doesn't. There is, naturally,
no scrap of conscious rivalry on Caroline's part; but those repressed
aspects of her released in the sado-masochistic Louis reveal well
enough how the need to worst Shirley is a subconscious component of the final settlement. Louis is introduced as a 'lower' Robert
so that Caroline can marry Robert himself yet leave Shirley a husband; Caroline rises to Shirley's role while Shirley descends to
marry someone much on Caroline's social level. The Louis–Shirley
union offers an obvious parallel to the Jane–Rochester relationship:
Louis, like Jane a private tutor, marries above him and will tame
his imperious spouse, but if he is Jane he is also in a sense Rochester, a dark, dominating figure who will cast Shirley in the role
of a meekly submissive Jane. In both novels, the 'lower' character
is able to exercise power because of a 'weakness' in the 'higher'
character: Rochester is crippled, Shirley is a woman. And since
Louis has been Shirley's tutor, his socially unequal relationship to
her is balanced by the spiritual superiority of being a teacher.
The 'Shirley' aspect of Caroline, then, finds fulfilment in Robert at
the same time as it is paradoxically transmuted through the figure
of Louis into the form of assuming power over Shirley herself.

In refusing Sir Philip Nunneley, Shirley deliberately flouts the
dynasticism of her outraged relatives and speaks up for Romantic
love. She rejects the Tory 'prejudices, aversions, dogmas' of Mr
Sympson:

Your god, sir, is the World. . . . Behold how hideously he governs! See him busied at the work he likes best – making

marriages. He binds the young to the old, the strong to the imbecile. He stretches out the arm of Mezentius and fetters the dead to the living. . . . Your god rules at the bridal of kings – look at your royal dynasties! Your deity is the deity of foreign aristocracies – analyze the blue blood of Spain![39]

The novel, however, does not allow Shirley to suffer for her liberalism. Her marriage with Louis triumphantly validates individual freedom while tying her closely to the flourishing fortunes of Louis's brother. It is no bad policy to align oneself as a landowner with the interests of the progressive bourgeoisie; Shirley has history on her side as well as conscience. As Caroline tells Robert Moore, Shirley's relationship with Louis 'is romantic, but it is also right'.[40] Like all Charlotte Brontë's novels, *Shirley* has in the end the best of both worlds. Its double-edged attitude to the Church – 'God save it! God also reform it!'[41] – is symptomatic of the compromising middle-ground which it attempts to occupy: a middle-ground between the most objectionable extremes of reverence and rebellion, land and trade, gentry and bourgeoisie.

# 4 Villette

When Jane Eyre turns on Mrs Reed, hotly accusing her of cruelty and neglect, she is quick to point out to the reader that her outburst is in no sense consciously calculated:

> 'What would uncle Reed say to you, if he were alive?' was my scarcely voluntary demand. I say scarcely voluntary, for it seemed as if my tongue pronounced words without my will consenting to their utterance: something spoke out of me over which I had no control.[1]

The novel needs to stress the 'scarcely voluntary' nature of Jane's denunciation, for to do otherwise would risk seriously damaging our image of her. Jane's comment is, indeed, dexterously cutting and well placed, accurately launched at her guardian's most vulnerable spot; and it is to avoid any suggestion of vindictiveness (not least on the part of a child) that the spontaneity of the remark is underlined. It is not the only place in Jane Eyre where the novelist resorts to such a device. A similar gambit is adopted when Jane, about to leave Lowood school, is pondering her future career:

> A kind fairy, in my absence, had surely dropped the required suggestion on my pillow; for as I lay down it came quietly and naturally to my mind: – 'Those who want situations advertise; you must advertise in the —shire Herald.'
> 'How? I know nothing about advertising.'
> Replies rose smooth and prompt now: —
> 'You must enclose the advertisement and the money to pay for it under a cover directed to the Editor of the Herald; you must put it, at the first opportunity you have, into the post at

Lowton; answers must be addressed to J.E. at the post-office there; you can go and inquire in about a week after you send your letter, if any are come, and act accordingly.'[2]

This brisk, unwittingly comic interior dialogue takes place between two facets of Jane: the meek, unworldly victim unable to act purposively, and the enterprising activist with an efficient knowledge of the measures essential for social advancement. That second Jane is repressed, depersonalised to a subconscious voice, sharply distinguished from the 'real' Jane who lacks the dynamism to succeed. The effect, then, is to show Jane moving eagerly forward without the objectionable implication that she is egoistically drafting her future. By the clumsy device of the divided self, Jane is able to make progress without detriment to her innocent passivity. Her return to Rochester is similarly engineered:

I saw nothing, but I heard a voice somewhere cry –
    'Jane! Jane! Jane!' nothing more.
    'O God! what is it?' I gasped.
    I might have said, 'Where is it?' for it did not seem in the room – nor in the house – nor in the garden; it did not come out of the air – nor from under the earth – nor from overhead. I had heard it – where, or whence, for ever impossible to know! And it was the voice of a human being – a known, loved, well-remembered voice – that of Edward Fairfax Rochester; and it spoke in pain and woe wildly, eerily, urgently.[3]

Lucy Snowe, the heroine of *Villette*, is also prompted to significant decisions by an involuntary power. It inspires her movement from the Midlands to London:

A bold thought was sent to my mind; my mind was made strong to receive it.
    'Leave this wilderness,' it was said to me, 'and go out hence.'
    'Where?' was the query.
    I had not very far to look; gazing from this country parish in that flat, rich middle of England – I mentally saw within reach what I had never yet beheld with my bodily eyes: I saw London.[4]

The same inner voice guides her to Villette and, having got her there, proves omniscient enough to know the precise residence she must visit: 'About a hundred thoughts volleyed through my mind in a moment. Yet I planned nothing, and considered nothing: I had not time. Providence said, 'Stop here; this is *your* inn.' Fate took me in her strong hand; mastered my will; directed my actions; I rang the door-bell.'⁵

This miraculous propulsion from point to point, in a process which will turn out to be one of social advancement, is enough to absolve Lucy from a charge of self-interested calculation; and it is an essential stratagem for resolving the Jane-like contradiction in her character. Lucy is presented to begin with as a spectatorial outsider; like Jane she is an alien in another's home, able to pride herself only on a coolly analytic brand of observation. 'I, Lucy Snowe, was calm',⁶ she declares, when neutrally recounting Polly Home's anguish at the departure of her father from the Bretton household. Yet her attitude towards the enigmatic Polly is intensely ambiguous: her heavily prosaic, taciturnly critical, Nelly Dean-like grimness with the girl (she is full of 'maxims of philosophy' with which to fend off Polly's tantalising blend of pertness and plangency) is so clearly self-defensive that it succeeds only in drawing attention to the firmly repressed fascination she feels for her more privileged, more emotionally vulnerable but also oddly opaque and self-possessed companion:

> I, Lucy Snowe, plead guiltless of that curse, an overheated and discursive imagination; but whenever, opening a room-door, I found her seated in a corner alone, her head in her pigmy hand, that room seemed to me not inhabited, but haunted.⁷

Lucy's attitude to Polly is, in fact, a subconscious tactical conversion of suppressed jealousy to mature condescension; a sort of malice is rationalised as a briskly commonsensical taking in hand. Polly is a 'little creature': she compares herself indirectly to a cat, as Ginevra Fanshawe is later compared spitefully to a mouse. She is spoilt, perverse but piquant, and so both resented and grudgingly admired. The capriciousness in her which attracts Graham Bretton suggests aspects of Lucy's own concealed emotional life; and in that sense Lucy's tight-lipped treatment of the girl signifies the erection of a blandly rational barrier against her own coldly unacknowledged impulses. Lucy projects herself into Polly and then coolly dissociates herself from that self-image, as indeed does

c*

Polly herself in public: 'Whilst lavishing her eccentricities regard-
lessly before me . . . she never showed my godmother one glimpse
of her inner self: for her, she was nothing but a docile, somewhat
quaint little maiden.'[8]

As a small but socially fortunate child, then, Polly is irritatingly
imperious but also touchingly helpless; and in this sense she reflects
a contradiction inherent in Lucy herself. Lucy, too, is both vulnerable and strenuously self-reliant, and the novel has to work hard
to preserve a balance between the two. She wants a sheltered life
in the Bretton household, even if this means sacrificing 'the charm
of variety . . . the excitement of incident';[9] she sees herself as
'prosaic', 'Tame and still by habit, disciplined by destiny',[10] and
feels the need of external stimulus to goad her into life:

> It seemed I must be stimulated into action. I must be goaded,
> driven, stung, forced to energy. . . . I had wanted to compromise
> with Fate: to escape occasional great agonies by submitting to a
> whole life of privation and small pains. Fate would not so be
> pacified; nor would Providence sanction this shrinking sloth and
> cowardly indolence.[11]

Is being forced into the wider world merely a harsh fate, inferior
to remaining obscurely cloistered, or is that shy withdrawal from
society really 'shrinking sloth and cowardly indolence', and
worldly progress therefore a positive good? Lucy herself is significantly unsure, finding herself friendless in London but also
enthralled by the turmoil of the City: ' "How is this?" said I. "Me-
thinks I am animated and alert, instead of being depressed and
apprehensive?" '[12] Miserable though she is on her first lonely night
in London, she has no wish to retract the step she has taken: 'A
strong, vague persuasion that it was better to go forward than
backward, and that I *could* go forward – that a way, however
narrow and difficult, would in time open – predominated over other
feelings. . . .'[13] Despite her insecurity, she has a proper scorn for
those bemused foreigners who marvel at the intrepidity of English
girls travelling alone.

As both enterprising individualist and helpless victim, Lucy is
caught in an interior conflict similar to Jane's. The trajectory of
both girls' careers is much the same: propelled from an initial
settlement into the promise and terror of independence, both need

to swallow back treacherous fantasies in the drive to carve a worldly niche. Yet Lucy is closer to William Crimsworth in her more articulate social ambition: 'unadventurous' though she declares herself, she also confesses contradictorily that her 'mind was a good deal bent on success'.[14] Passivity and self-denial bring social benefits in all of Charlotte's novels, as Lucy discovers in a minor way when she first encounters snobbish servants in a London inn: 'Maintaining a very quiet manner towards this arrogant little maid, and subsequently observing the same towards the parsonic-looking, black-coated, white-neckclothed waiter, I got civility from them ere long.'[15] But whereas in *Jane Eyre* this truth remains secretively implicit, the unilluminated underside of the novel, Lucy Snowe is allowed to formulate it into an explicit project for self-advancement: 'Courage, Lucy Snowe! With self-denial and economy now, and steady exertion by-and-by, an object in life need not fail you.'[16]

Lucy's internal contradictions can be charted most clearly in her thoroughly ambiguous attitude towards her employer, Madame Beck. Madame Beck is a spying, scheming little bourgeoise who privately examines the contents of Lucy's luggage when she first arrives; but Lucy is notably generous in her excusal of this action. ('Her duty done – I felt that in her eyes this business was a duty – she rose, noiselessly as a shadow....')[17] The text of the novel is jumpily unpredictable in its variations of hostility and approbation: Madame Beck's watchwords are 'Surveillance, espionage',[18] yet she knows what honesty is – 'that is, when it did not intrude its clumsy scruples in the way of her will and interest'.[19] She seems to know that keeping girls in restraint and blind ignorance is not the best way to educate them, and we are about to applaud her liberalism when we learn her opinion that 'ruinous consequences would ensue if any other method were tried with continental children'.[20] Her system is 'easy, liberal, salutary, and rational',[21] yet we hear later that she rears minds in Romish slavery; she is 'Wise, firm, faithless, secret, crafty',[22] but is judged by Lucy to be 'a very great and a very capable woman'[23] – until, that is, she is finally exposed as a thorough villain. If the reader is at a loss to know what to make of Madame Beck, the novel itself seems equally mystified.

That bemusement has its root in Lucy's own vacillating response to her superior – vacillating because Madame Beck is at once her

oppressor and an image of the icy rational power she herself
wants to possess. Her spying is naturally resented, but it also stirs
Lucy's Romantic sensibilities: Madame Beck's noiseless gliding
about the school reminds us of the equally elusive 'ghost', to
whom Lucy reacts with a similar compound of commonsensical
scorn and covert fascination. Like her school, Madame Beck is a
curious mixture of rational benevolence and oppressive restraint;
her stoical self-composure appeals to Lucy's own dourly rationalist streak, but its tantalising opacity is also imaginatively
seductive.

Madame Beck's frigid calm, then, is both criticised and
approved; and indeed the novel's categorial structure is built
chiefly around a set of oppositions between calm and storm, calculative rationalism and Romantic impulse, self-possession and
emotional self-exposure. Lucy lives at the focal point of these
tensions, and their resolution is to be found in the figure of her
fiery little lover, Paul Emmanuel. ('Little' is significant: Paul is
domineering but, like Hunsden, physically slight, as Madame Beck,
conversely, appears occasionally like a man.) Fiery though he is,
Paul is also puritanically austere, and so provides Lucy with precisely the right amalgam of passion and censoriousness. He is, in
fact, a kind of Hunsden, scoffing but covertly a soul-mate, caustic
but secretly charitable. Like Madame Beck he is a sly intriguer, but
unlike her he is turbulent, impetuous and hair-raisingly ferocious
into the bargain.

Rumour has it that Paul was educated by Jesuits, and Jesuits,
as the fearful epitome of Roman Catholicism for Charlotte, are
associated at once with worldly deviousness and ascetic absolutism,
manipulative cunning and cloak-and-dagger Romance. Since the
quarrel between worldly and ascetic forms of religion is an important one in Charlotte's fiction, not least in its treatment of Evangelicalism, it is worth adding a digressive note on it here. In so
far as Evangelicalism sets out to crush the Romantic spirit, it is
a tangible symbol of social violence and must be resisted. Jane
Eyre rebels against Brocklehurst's cruel cant and Rivers's deathly
Calvinism; she also scorns Eliza Reed's decision to enter a Roman
Catholic convent, viewing this as a falsely ascetic withdrawal from
the world. But she is at the same time 'Quakerish' herself, grimly
disapproving of worldly libertinism; and in this sense she is torn

between respect for and instinctive distrust of stringent religious discipline, caught between pious submission and defiant rebellion. Charlotte Brontë's attitudes to Evangelicalism are, in short, thoroughly ambiguous, as is obvious enough if the detestable Brocklehurst is placed in the balance against the treatment of spoilt children in the novels, where evangelical attitudes to childhood strongly emerge. The theme of pampered, perverse children crops up in almost all the Brontës' novels, and the evangelical responses involved with it are clearly, in part, class-responses: exasperated reactions to the indolent offspring of the rich, as in Anne Brontë's talk of the need to crush vicious tendencies in the bud in the Bloomfield family scenes of *Agnes Grey*. It is an evangelical impulse to avoid 'cowardly indolence' and sally out instead to put one's soul to the test which motivates Lucy's journey to Villette; it is a similar impulse which brings Caroline Helstone to reject as false, Romish superstition the idea that virtue lies in self-abnegation, and decide instead to become a governess. What Hunsden sees as attractive 'spirit' in Crimsworth's son Victor, Crimsworth himself interprets as 'the leaven of the offending Adam',[24] and considers that it should be, if not whipped out of him, at least soundly disciplined.

Evangelical discipline, then, is hateful in its sour oppressiveness but useful in curbing the libertine, over-assertive self. It is to be rejected in so far as, like Rivers's Calvinism, it turns one away from the world, but welcomed as a spur to worldly effort and achievement. At the same time, religion can clearly be *too* worldly; and this is true in *Villette* of Roman Catholicism, whose clergy are condemned as 'mitred aspirants for this world's kingdoms'.[25] On the other hand, the Roman Church is despised with healthy, rational, Protestant contempt for its lurid superstition and primitive otherworldliness; and in this ambivalence it becomes a microcosm of the 'foreign' in general. Belgium in *Villette* is portrayed as a flat, drab expanse people by dreary, lumpish bourgeois, a mundane and materialist enclave; but it is also a land of mystery and imbroglio, of plotting, drugging and haunting. The 'foreign' in Charlotte's fiction offers an imaginative adventure absent at home: its very alienness converts it to a blank surface on to which private fantasies may be feverishly projected. Yet since that alienness is entwined with spying and oppression, it intensifies the

claustrophobic home environment as well as providing an escape
from it.

What Paul Emmanuel represents, in effect, is an agreeable combination of Hunsden and Frances Henri, as his lecture in the
*Tribune* reveals:

> Who would have thought the flat and fat soil of Labasse-
> cour could yield political convictions and national feelings,
> such as were now strongly expressed? Of the bearing of his
> opinions I need here give no special indication: yet it may be
> permitted me to say I believed the little man not more earnest
> than right in what he said: with all his fire he was severe and
> sensible; he trampled Utopian theories under his heels; he re-
> jected wild dreams with scorn; – but, when he looked in the face
> of tyranny – oh, then there opened a light in his eye worth see-
> ing; and when he spoke of injustice, his voice gave no uncertain
> sound, but reminded me rather of the band-trumpet, ringing at
> twilight from the park.[26]

Paul unites a 'sensible' anti-radicalism with fiery reformist zeal,
Protestant rationalism with Catholic spirit; if he shares Frances
Henri's conservative patriotism, he also has something of Hunsden's
scorching contempt for political reaction. He is a man 'always
somewhat shy at meeting the advances of the wealthy'[27] and, like
Lucy, has known poverty, having starved for a year in a Rome
garret. Because he is passionate himself, he alone can appreciate
the true Lucy behind the protective façade; he sees shrewdly that
her calm conceals a storm like his, and believes consequently in
chastising her: 'You want so much checking, regulating, and keeping down.'[28] Lucy finds the discipline energising, and is flattered
that one man at least has intuited her hidden imaginative depths
in a society which obtusely takes her skilfully contrived sang-
froid at face-value. Paul's censoriousness, then, is not merely that
of a hard-headed English Protestant grimly extirpating the sin of
fancy, although Lucy welcomes it as a curb to her guilty imaginings; it also imputes to her a vivacity and inner complexity to
which others are dully insensitive, and so reveals Paul's own
attractive subtlety of perception. In so far as it is part of Paul's
Jesuitism, it is at least as impressive a form of despotism as
Madame Beck's crafty schemings. Both Roman Catholicism and

Protestantism, in fact combine rigorous self-discipline with imaginative intensity: Lucy speaks of Methodist and Papist as equally fantastical, and indeed the Romish tract which Paul gives her reminds her of Wesleyan pamphlets read in childhood.

Paul tells Lucy at one point that she needs 'watching, and watching over',[29] and that verbal conjunction says much about their relationship. Being watched is objectionable, but in so far as it involves being watched over – cared for – it is clearly desirable. To be critically scrutinised by another at least implies a negative form of interest on his part, perhaps the most you can hope for in a hostile, treacherous society. Paul's constant secret surveillance of all the school's inmates from his lattice-window links him closely to the oppressive world of Villette but also lends him a seductive air of divinity, raises him above routine pettiness and plotting. Even so, Lucy does not allow herself to be seduced without a struggle. When she finds Paul 'sullying the shield of Britannia, and dabbling the union-jack in the mud' in the course of a particularly vitriolic harangue to his students, she is quickly stung to chauvinist contempt for 'these clowns of Labassecour', striking her desk with a resounding cry of 'Vive l'Angleterre, l'Histoire et les Héros!'[30] It is Frances and Hunsden once more, but the conflict is this time more complex. For whereas Frances is simply a conservative patriot, Lucy is also a latent rebel; and it is the latency of that rebelliousness which constitutes one of the most interesting features of *Villette*. It emerges most obviously in her ambiguous attitude towards the Bretton family, and especially towards the alluring young John. The Brettons have the genuine sang-froid of which Lucy's coolness is a contrived, self-protective parody; and as such they win from her a kind of admiring envy. She feels unable to recount her harrowing experiences to Mrs Bretton because of the difference of circumstance between them:

The difference between her and me might be figured by that between the stately ship cruising safe on smooth seas, with its full complement of crew, a captain gay and brave, and venturous and provident; and the life-boat, which most days of the year lies dry and solitary in an old, dark boat-house, only putting to sea when the billows run high in rough weather,

when cloud encounters water, when danger and death divide
between them the rule of the great deep.[31]

The contrast goes formally in Mrs Bretton's favour: respectable
women of her kind are not to be affronted by sordid tales of
mental anguish. She is, Lucy comments elsewhere, 'an English
middle-class gentlewoman'[32] — English' making the difference, since
the Belgian burghers are universally despised. Yet the novel has
constantly to repress under this 'official' attitude a flickering resentment of that English bourgeois blandness epitomised by the Brettons and gratifyingly absent in Paul.

Lucy's view of John Bretton, for example, grows stealthily more
critical as the novel develops, without ever declaring itself directly.
The play staged at the school under Paul's direction is a case in
point. Lucy plays a foppish male wooer of Ginevra Fanshawe, the
coquette with whom John is in love; and the fact that John is in
the audience spurs her on to 'woo' Ginevra from him. She does
this because she herself loves John and wants to separate him from
Ginevra; but since she is also symbolically competing with Bretton,
the act expresses at the same time a certain oblique antagonism
to him. Her 'wooing' of Ginevra is equally double-edged: it releases
her hostility to the girl, since its aim is to divorce her from Bretton,
but also signifies a grudging admiration for Ginevra's success
and an impulse to identify with her. (Ginevra, she discovers later,
is gradually becoming for her a kind of heroine, even though she
sees this to be an illusion; despite her 'plain prose knowledge' of
the empty-headed Society flirt, 'a kind of reflected glow began to
settle on her idea'.)[33] Since Lucy loves the man who loves Ginevra,
there is a sense in which she loves Ginevra too; and since Ginevra
treats Lucy in the play as a substitute John, Lucy is out to attract
her. In so far as Lucy's behaviour suggests a desire to oust Ginevra
from John's affections but also to unlodge John from Ginevra's,
it reveals her ambiguous approval and resentment of those more
successful than herself. It implies a loving concern for Bretton
and a competitive jealousy of him, a fascination with Ginevra and
a desire to injure her.*

* The sexual complexities of the situation are particularly knotty: Lucy,
a passionate woman with a dominative streak, plays an effeminate man,
wooing a 'feminine' yet imperious girl to win her from a strong male weakly
under her power.

Lucy has commented sharply in an early aside that she thought the young John thoroughly spoilt; and she is certainly irritated later by the absurdity of his love for Ginevra. She is also ready to admit that he is cruelly vain, lacks sympathetic warmth and is in some ways emotionally shallow; but at the same time his very incapacity for emotional turbulence contrasts favourably with Paul's choler. John offers rest and refuge; but the novel, while like all Charlotte's work deeply committed to a dream of placid self-fulfilment, also has a needling animus against it – the animus of the socially inferior whose lot is to suffer distraction and despair. John is 'a cheerful fellow by nature',[34] and soon recovers from Ginevra's rejection of him; but this resilience, while in a sense applauded, also reveals that lack of complex emotional depth which leads him to see Lucy herself superficially:

> 'I wish I could tell [Polly] all I recall; or rather, I wish some one, *you* for instance, would go behind and whisper it all in her ear, and I could have the delight – here, as I sit – of watching her look under the intelligence. Could you manage that, think you, Lucy, and make me ever grateful?'
> 'Could I manage to make you ever grateful?' said I. 'No, *I could not.*' And I felt my fingers work and my hands interlock: I felt, too, an inward courage, warm and resistant. In this matter I was not disposed to gratify Dr John: not at all. With now welcome force, I realized his entire misapprehension of my character and nature. He wanted always to give me a rôle not mine. Nature and I opposed him. He did not at all guess what I felt: he did not read my eyes, or face, or gestures; though, I doubt not, all spoke. Leaning towards me coaxingly, he said softly, '*Do* content me, Lucy'.[35]

The passage teeters on the edge of a sardonic poke at John's sentimental egoism, but just manages to repress its tartness. A page later, we are back to eulogising the dashing young doctor: 'Dr John, throughout his whole life, was a man of luck – a man of success. And why? Because he had the eye to see his opportunity, the heart to prompt to well-timed action, the nerve to consummate a perfect work. . . .'[36] This, indeed, is the final, 'official' verdict; the novel's subcurrent of resentment, stemmed by the overriding need to celebrate bourgeois security, is for-

bidden to break disruptively through the book's surface. Lucy's
bitterness at John's breezy treatment of her is clearly a class-
issue – 'Had Lucy been intrinsically the same, but possessing
the additional advantages of wealth and station, would your
manner to her, your value for her, have been quite what they
actually were?'[37] – but it is a bitterness prudently quelled. The
smooth, stately life-style of a Mrs Bretton, subconscious irritant
though it may be to the poor and dispossessed, symbolises none
the less a point of aspiration and stability which must at all costs
be preserved.

Even so, the novel's option to unite Lucy to Paul rather than
John speaks eloquently enough. (Lucy loses nothing socially by
this move, of course, since Paul is of a wealthy background and
John is not of aristocratic stock.) The opposition between the
two men is one between convention and eccentricity, domesticity
and solitariness, the English and the alien, gentility and passion;
but those tensions are contained and negotiated by the book's
refusal to allow a Rochester–Rivers kind of confrontation between
them. *Villette* is in some ways a more tragic work than *Jane Eyre*,
but it is also more accommodating, more concerned to muffle
direct antagonism. Like Jane, Lucy lives as a child in someone else's
household, but unlike Jane she is 'a good deal taken notice of';[38]
and since she is therefore less of an exile she is less ready to rebel.
The world is to be temporised with rather than subversively
challenged; Lucy maintains, against Ginevra Fanshawe's jejune
snobbery, that pedigree and social position are of minor
importance, but 'The world, I soon learned, held a different
estimate: and I make no doubt, the world is very right in its view,
yet believe also that I am not quite wrong in mine.'[39] That 'not
quite wrong' proves ominous: as Lucy goes on to tease out the
contradiction, the balance tips quietly on the side of the world.

The tensions are also contained by the fact that Paul Emmanuel,
like Shirley and unlike Hunsden, is a rebel more in style than
substance. He may be tempestuously individualist, but it is he
who is morally outraged to find Lucy viewing a nude portrait in a
local art-gallery, and she who is thereby cast into the role of
quirkily independent Englishwoman. Lucy's response to the portrait is significant: it embodies a crude, overblown naturalism,
and her distaste for it suggests a cultural superiority to the

prosiac Belgians at the same time as it manifests a brusquely commonsensical English philistinism. There is a similar ambivalence in her reaction to the theatrical performance to which Bretton takes her: she finds it at once stupendous and sordid. ('It was a marvellous sight: a mighty revelation. It was a spectacle low, horrible, immoral.'⁴⁰) English-puritan and European-Romantic jostle each other uneasily; indeed, one of their rare points of fusion in the novel is in the figure of Polly's father, Mr Home, who is part Scots and part French aristocrat, 'at once proud-looking and homely-looking',⁴¹ combining Gallic grace with Scots ruggedness. In a telling irony, one of the few admirable European aristocrats in the book (French, significantly, rather than lumpishly Belgian) turns out to be partly Scots.

Moreover, Paul Emmanuel does finally offer Lucy, as Rochester ultimately offers Jane, both emotional fulfilment *and* a sheltered refuge. He sets her up in business as a private teacher, providing her with a well-appointed residence. The ambiguity of the novel's ending – is Paul drowned or not? – is then appropriate to the book's continually double-edged attitude to the question of secure settlement. Even on the brink of disaster, happiness is not allowed to be wholly snatched away; it survives as an ideal possibility which might validate the suffering channelled into its achievement. Yet suffering, on the other hand, is too palpable to be merely swallowed up into felicity; and so the conclusion remains calculatedly unresolved, underlining the delights of domestic settlement at the same time as it protests against the bland unreality of such an ending, witnessing to the truth of an emotional agony which cannot be simply wished away. In the end, the novel is unable to opt for either possibility: it cannot betray its sense of the reality of failure, but swerves nervously away from the corollary that this might imply – that worldly achievement may be empty and invalid. In the end, *Villette* has neither the courage to be tragic nor to be comic; like all of Charlotte's novels, although in its conclusion more obviously than any, it is a kind of middle-ground, a half-measure.

# 5 The Structure of Charlotte Brontë's Fiction

I have tried in the previous chapters to disengage from the textual density of Charlotte Brontë's fiction a certain informing structure. I want now to examine that structure more generally, and to consider its relevance to some questions of literary form and value in the novels.

The fundamental structure of Charlotte's novels is a triadic one: it is determined by a complex play of power-relations between a protagonist, a 'Romantic-radical' and an autocratic conservative. In *Jane Eyre* these roles are fulfilled respectively by Jane, Rochester and St John Rivers; in *The Professor* by William Crimsworth, Yorke Hunsden and Edward Crimsworth; in *Shirley* by Caroline Helstone, Shirley Keeldar and Robert Moore; and in *Villette* by Lucy Snowe, Paul Emmanuel and Madame Beck. That structure is rarely *neatly* triadic: a particular function may be shared between two or more characters, just as in *Shirley* the Romantic-radical figure is chiefly Shirley herself, but also in a sense the Carlylean hero Moore.

In no case, indeed, is it a question of a *simple* informing structure. On the contrary, we discover in each work an inherently complex system where roles are fluid and permutable, where characters may embody degrees of fusion and overlapping between two or more functions. And this lability of the structure, which allows roles to be combined, displaced and inverted within a controlling order of literary types, is a major clue to the novels' meaning. The primary structural relationship, of which each work is a unique mutation, holds between two characters who are *both* blends of conformism and rebelliousness, but where one stands in deferential relation to the dominative other. This is the case with Jane and Rochester, Crimsworth and Hunsden, Caroline and Shirley, Lucy and Paul. Both dominative and deferential figures are self-divided, torn between criticism and endorsement of social orthodoxy; and the upshot is less a straight confrontation between two types than a shifting pattern of conflict and affinity between four *personae*. Because the figures in each pair are unequal, the 'lower' character (who is always the protagonist) can find in the 'higher' both an emulable image of achievement and an agreeable reflection of his or her own deviant individualism. This latter facet of the higher figure is subtly attractive to the protagonist, yet also affronts her* wary conservatism – a conservatism which seems as inevitable a posture as dissent in the subservient figure seeking recognition in a hostile society. The superior character, in turn, fulfils himself by punishing and protecting his partner, but delights in the energising enmity which this generates; he finds in her, as she finds in him, a fascinating interplay of affinity and otherness.

Because the heroine finds both solace and perverse stimulation in her superior, the final resolution contains a contention between them which fulfils several ends. It underwrites the heroine's impulse for independent identity in a depersonalising world; it allows her to vent a suppressed resentment of the other which is for the most part a function of class-bitterness; and it thereby partly purges her of the guilt of rebelliousness. It achieves all these ends, moreover, without threatening that secure dependency which furnishes these conflicts with a stable context. The heroine's lonely *self*-reproval is replaced by a glad submission to the censorings of a soul-mate – censorings which stimulate rather than crush the spirit. The sexual expression of this transaction, as I have tried to show, is sado-masochism. Energy and discipline, freedom and obedience, conformity and individualism cease to be antithetical and merge into mythical unity.

The tension between 'Romance' and 'realism' which I have traced in my account of the novels is merely another metaphor for the workings of this structure. 'Romance', I am aware, is a crudely inadequate term; but I mean by it merely the passionate

---

* I shall refer to the protagonist as 'her', for the sake of convenience, although most of what I have to say includes Crimsworth too.

self's free, eloquent expression, in contrast to that calculative rationalism which I designate as 'realism' – the analytic adequation of means to ends in the name of worldly progress. All the 'higher' characters are Romantic in this sense: they manifest a rich fluency of selfhood, a flair, *brio* and flamboyance which in its overriding of rationalist meanness wins the heroine's envying wonder. The heroine admires this life-style because she lives it also – but lives it as guilty secret, as submerged, unspeakable fantasy. She needs to negotiate her own undeclared Romanticism in terms of a real world; and to do that calls into play the opposing values of pragmatic analysis and effort. It is important to see that each of these aspects of the self-divided heroine can be radical and conservative in turn. Romantic emotion, guiltily thrust back on itself, becomes a smothered protest against a society which by denying vision distorts it into billowing fantasy; and in the 'higher' figure it emerges as a vivaciously radical *panache*. But at the same time the full gush of that emotion is typically channelled into a heady celebration of the heroic, a lurid, slipshod exaltation of the patriotic, the traditionalist, the doggedly provincial. As such, the novels assume their place within a nineteenth-century tradition of radical conservatism, upbraiding a niggardly rationalistic capitalism in the name of individualist verve and fading chivalric virtue.

'Realism' contains an equal political ambivalence. It emerges on the one hand as a critical, clear-sighted refusal to be mystified by the regalia of rank and despotic power; and as such it incarnates a liberal-egalitarian ethic, progressive in its scorn of upper-class privilege and cant, intimately responsive to the solid, sober and suffering. But its most salient feature is bourgeois ambition, cloaked and unconfessed to various degrees – an ambition which, while fiercely contesting the system which denies it full growth, inevitably takes that system as its cherished end. The structure of Charlotte's fiction, then, must achieve an appropriate balance between nostalgic reaction and forward-looking enterprise – or, conversely, between Romantic *panache* and realist prudence. In searching out that point of balance, the novels, as I have argued, are attuned to a real history: their ideological interplay has its source in a pattern of conflicts and alignments between contemporary social classes.

The categorial structure of an author's world is not to be confused with that organised distribution of technical devices to which we traditionally give the name of literary form. Lucien Goldmann, from whom I derive the notion of categorial structure, sometimes seems to use the term synonymously with the formal structure of a text; but this, surely, is to by-pass a genuine aesthetic problem. What is the relation between the 'structure' of an author's world-view and the 'structure' of his fiction? My own view is that the second is a mediated embodiment of the first – that a categorial structure creates or refashions the literary forms appropriate to it, and that 'form' is in that sense a consequence of 'structure'. Not, of course, a mere epiphenomenon of structure. Charlotte Brontë, like any author, inherited a complex, relatively autonomous legacy of literary forms, but only some of these forms sufficed to articulate her ideological vision. The history of literary form is not merely a shorthand way of writing the history of literary consciousness; but the two are none the less leashed together by an internal bond. I want now to examine briefly some of the formal elements which crystallise out the 'deep' structure of Charlotte's fiction, and this will involve raising a question which I have so far deliberately put in parentheses: the question of the novels' relative literary value.

The narrative form of all Charlotte's novels, with the exception of *Shirley*, is first-person; but some are, as it were, more first-person than others. *The Professor*, for example, is recounted in the first person, but it is really in a sense a third-person narration. Crimsworth delivers his success-story externally, judiciously, treating himself as the admirable object of his own narration; and although we are of course given access to his consciousness, it is remarkably even and unruffled compared with the throttled-back torments of a Jane, Caroline or Lucy. What we learn about Crimsworth, indeed, is less what he is conscious of than what he is unconscious of: it is the absences and evasions in his narrative, the unilluminated underside of his story, which speak most eloquently – absences he cannot know himself because he has stripped himself of all but the most marginal self-reflection, objectified himself so efficiently to a third person. There is a sense in which we have most vital access to Crimsworth precisely at the points where he most crucially lacks access to himself. In the other novels we dis-

cover a sharp dichotomy between self and society, the stuff of interior fantasy and the material world; but though this is fleet-
ingly present in *The Professor* it is only notionally there, the mere
ghost of a dualism. The chief formal problem of all Charlotte's
novels is how to resolve the tension between 'Romance' and
'realism' – to resolve it not only as *theme* but as *writing*. *The
Professor* 'solves' this problem at a stroke by suppressing the
secret recesses of anguish and self-doubt, choosing instead a mode
of subjectivity which tends to absolute control over an apparently
recalcitrant but in the end magically pliant world. The novel is
really Crimsworth's tribute to himself – the record of a first-
person narrator who sees himself as laudably capable and impas-
sive third person. We are meant to regard Crimsworth much as
Mdlle Reuter regards him, and as he views himself in the mirror
of her glance; and it is because he is unconsciously present to himself as a third person that he can hand himself plaudits with no
sense of smugness. The cool, economical narrative is itself an index
of his edge over the world; the whole action is resolutely externalised, the brisk, even, bloodless style in marked contrast to the
tumid, erratic prose we occasionally encounter in the other works.
It is as though, from the dense complexities of those works, a
single, stark graph of development (isolation, enterprise, final
settlement) has been surgically extracted, trimmed of the entanglements with which it is involved elsewhere. In this sense *The Professor* is the blueprint of Charlotte's fiction; it muffles the
conflicts apparent in other works, not by dreaming up a Romantic
ideal (a Shirley, for instance), but by creating a character whose
very prosaicness equips him for survival and success. It is one
drastic strategy for worsting the world, demanding little less than
the calculated surrender of imaginative awareness. For the novel
fully to admit the experience of suffering and solitude into its
world would be for it to risk collapse; it is only by a constant
deflection of those facts that it survives. Low-keyed and cool-
temperatured as it is, *The Professor* is loud with the human
truths it smothers; it is the very unshakeability of Crimsworth's
composure, its sustained, uncrackable contrivance, which persuades
us of the fundamental anxiety lurking unconfessed behind it.

The novel's apparently crass insensitivity to its hero's complacency – to the fact that he is, unknown to himself or (it appears)

the novel, a thoroughly unlikeable character – signifies well enough what the book has to sacrifice, what delicacies of feeling it has to blunt to bring off this one-dimensional piece of wish-fulfilment. But 'unlikeable' is perhaps a misplaced term: we are invited neither to like nor dislike Crimsworth, only to follow his upward social trek with interest and respect. Affection and repulsion are luxuries in the society which Crimsworth is forced to confront; Hunsden, for instance, seems incapable of actually speaking his friendship for the Professor. Like all Charlotte's protagonists, Crimsworth must make himself invulnerable to others; but what is remarkable about the novel is that 'others', for these purposes, includes the reader too. Not even the reader must be allowed to slip under his guard; and this is why in reading his narrative we have the exasperated sense that he is telling us only what he wants us to know – gilding a fact here, rationalising an attitude there, passing laconically over a crucial interlude. Crimsworth is a manifestly untrustworthy narrator: he treats the reader with something like the stiff, wary circumspection with which he handles Mdlle Reuter. The first, quickly abandoned narrative device the novel uses is an epistolary one: Crimsworth opens his autobiography in the form of a letter to a former school-friend, and begins that letter by wondering aloud to his correspondent why he is writing to *him*. Though they shared an affinity at school, they were temperamental opposites. The reader is then effectively placed in the correspondent's position: we wonder too, reserved and unspontaneous as he is, quite why Crimsworth is writing to us, and so, we sense, does he.

I have implied that the novel's treatment of its hero is wholly unironic, which is not exactly true; it is certainly difficult, for example, to imagine the book's entirely straight-faced endorsement of William's bloodthirsty urge to whip old Adam out of his son. But neither is it true that the treatment is ironic; the novel seems instead to inhabit some third, less easily definable category. The smugly unselfcritical way in which Crimsworth is presented seems itself an act of half-conscious defiance on the novel's part – an unspoken insistence that we take his behaviour on the constrictive terms of his society, appealing to other sources of value by which to judge him. In that case, what is ironic about *The Professor* is nothing less than the total novel: it is a fraction of Charlotte's world which offers itself as a whole. The smooth exclusion of other values is itself a kind of structural irony – an essential rigour which we must either take or leave, rather as Crimsworth himself toughly rationalises his miserable treatment of Frances as a necessary tutorial strictness concealing hidden depths of affection. If this is the case, then it may be that the book is playing a curious, complicated game with the reader, akin to Crimsworth's sadistic sport with Frances. It shows us the least engaging traits of its hero but does so in an oddly unapologetic way, as though to remind us that these are the harshly essential terms on which to work. It is as if the book is half-aware of its protagonist's flaws but resolves to appear oblivious of them – grimly refuses to render him personable, and so obliquely raises the question of those narrowing limits, banishing affection and interiority, within which both novel and hero are compelled to move.

If *The Professor* conceals a third-person narration beneath its autobiographical form, *Shirley*, a third-person novel, secretes a tacitly first-person narration – that of Caroline Helstone – within it. The choice of the third-person form is logical enough for a novel which offers itself in part as a kind of social documentary; but it is the lack of structural symmetry between this aspect of the work and the 'first-person' Romance woven into it which accounts for a good deal of the book's formal diffuseness. The 'social realist' and 'Romantic' dimensions of the work are loosely conjoined in the figure of Robert Moore, whose blindness to all but profit both motivates the Luddite assault and throws Caroline into emotional turmoil; but there is a significant reason why the two issues, public and private, are unable genuinely to interact. The reason is that, in contrast with, say, the relationship between Jane and Rochester, there is no class-conflict between Caroline and Moore. Whereas *Jane Eyre* weaves together its social and sexual combats with an impressive degree of success, *Shirley*, a novel much preoccupied with middle-class solidarity in the face of the proletarian enemy, has effectively to split off personal tensions into the arena of private Romance. There is, then, an ideological determination for this formal flaw. In *The Professor*, the social issue predominates damagingly over the personal: Crimsworth can easily discard his brother Edward on social grounds, and Frances is the ideally privatised Victorian wife. In *Villette*, Paul Emmanuel's foreignness renders him effectively classless in English eyes, so that the themes of rebellion, conformity and resentment are displaced into primarily sexual terms. In *Shirley*, however, social and sexual antagonisms are politically forbidden to cross-breed; and in this sense the book's amorphous form results not from an uncontrolled exposure of conflicts which shatter its framework (a point which might justly be made about *Villette*), but from exactly the opposite: from a certain suppression of social contradictions among its major characters. Caroline, for instance, has liberal objections to Moore's ruling-class ruthlessness, but these become muted as the novel progresses and nowhere seriously complicate a primarily sexual problem. Her relationship with Shirley similarly lacks social friction: she never questions her social inferiority to her companion. Caroline's relation to both 'higher' characters therefore lacks the enriching ingredient of social contention common to the relations of Jane and Rochester, Crimsworth and Hunsden, Lucy and Bretton; and indeed this is obvious in the very device of introducing Shirley early into the novel. Whereas the other works move dynamically through friction to resolution, Shirley broods over the action as a sublime resolution in herself, and so forestalls any significant evolution. Unlike Rochester, Hunsden and Bretton she is a flawless ideal, a paradigm of the desirable reconciliation who, by prematurely foreclosing the process of social conflict, diffuses the narrative to a fragmented sequence of portraits, vignettes, dramatic interludes. Unlike Jane and Lucy, Caroline can achieve in the present an unqualified fulfilment with the 'higher' figure; and this deprives the novel of dramatic thrust, rendering it unsatisfyingly episodic. There is a parallel kind of prematurity in Caroline's early discovery of her lost mother Mrs Pryor; this too is a move to assuage her *Angst* now rather than later, and so to slacken the force of that Jane-like drive which might bear her beyond a familiar social landscape to a world outside. Jane, Crimsworth and Lucy are prised out of their domestic enclaves; Caroline is supplied with palliatives to keep her where she is. The typical Charlotte tale of a solitary heroine is concealed at the core of *Shirley*, but within an assuring context which robs it of narrative dynamic. For all her unslaked longing, Caroline inhabits a social world which is essentially *hers*, and from which dramatic disengagement is therefore unnecessary. In so far as Caroline projects on to Shirley feelings unreciprocated by the coldly ideological Moore, Shirley figures in part as a 'personal' alternative to the 'social' realm. Shirley does of course play a public role herself, but it seems for the most part little more than an extension of her personal charisma. Since she conflates the personal and social, there is no possibility of Caroline's encountering a conflict between them in their relationship. In this sense Caroline differs from Jane and Crimsworth, whose affection for their superiors is complicated by significant reservations. The novel separates personal and social themes in distinguishing Shirley from Moore, but merges them in the person of Shirley herself; and these, indeed, are logically related moves. In the absence of an adequately dialectical grasp of the relations in question, conflation becomes the crudely obvious tactic for surmounting dichotomy. Caroline's involvement with Moore forces the two dimensions apart, her friendship with Shirley runs them romantically together, and both strategies spring from a suppression of social antagonism. Moore destructively divorces the social and personal, and Shirley serves as an implicit critique of that blunder; but because in her case the two realms are reduced to one, the social diminished to a mere embodiment of personal spirit, the implication is that the difference between her and Moore is largely one of personality.

I have argued that *Villette* smooths the edge of a social criticism by transmuting it into sexual conflict – a move which leaves orthodox society intact, yet turns from it to a more fertile centre of commitment. Caroline's social disagreements with Moore, as we have seen, are similarly muted; but then, in a double suppression, her counterposing relationship with Shirley is also emptied of strife. This is so because the relationship is (consciously, at least) asexual, but also because Shirley as capitalist is a 'higher' type of Moore and so defends rather than opposes him. She is closer ideologically to Moore than she is to the radical Yorke – an affinity sealed by the fact that Moore is a hybrid of Hunsden and Edward Crimsworth, secreting a Romantic spirit behind his inflexible exterior. The 'higher' characters of other works mix Romantic conservatism with a spice of iconoclasm, but Shirley's nonconformity reduces itself pretty much to a matter of personal style (she whistles, for example). The privileged alliance between master and heroine in other works is both a respite from struggle and full of enthralling strife, since the master is both revered and mischievously repulsed; in *Shirley* it is merely a matter of reverence.

In *Jane Eyre* the choice between 'Romantic' and 'rationalist' is clear-cut: Jane rejects Rivers and opts for Rochester.* In *The Professor* the issue is slightly more complex: Crimsworth plumps for the 'Romantic' Hunsden against the hard-headed Edward, but since Hunsden is hardly dewy-eyed himself, a counterpointing commitment to Frances proves essential. The fusing of qualities within one role generates the need for another. *Villette* selects Paul as a partner for Lucy and rejects Bretton, but though these two commitments are in a sense incompatible, the novel shrinks from an absolute decision between them. This also holds true for *Shirley*, but with an important difference: for here Shirley and Moore represent nothing like a significant opposition. Shirley is clearly the Romantic, and Moore broadly the 'rationalist' figure, but they are to be simultaneously possessed rather than placed in the balance. This is partly accomplished by the distribution of sexual roles: since Shirley is a woman, Caroline cannot actually unite with her but needs a sexual partner, rather as Crimsworth needs Frances. *The Professor*, however, sustains a conflict between Frances and Hunsden, as Jane is torn between two suitors and Lucy divided between John and Paul. *Shirley*, on the other hand, lacks these bracing tensions: what strife there is in the novel, apart from pitched battles with the proletariat, is confined to a maladjustment between Caroline and her environment. Her claustrophobia does, of course, raise the 'woman question', but this is relatively detached from the novel's social fabric; and it is not even concretised in outright hostility to her authoritarian guardian Helstone. Stiff-necked as he is, Helstone is not an Edward Crimsworth, Brocklehurst or Madame Beck: the novel's compulsive sense of class-solidarity extends to him too.

At root, then, Shirley and Moore are complementary rather

* The roles themselves, of course, are considerably less clear-cut: both men combine 'Romance' and 'rationalism' in differently proportioned measures.

than contradictory types. When Caroline sees them walking together, they seem to her 'two great happy spirits', soul-mates
who should marry; and one of the effects of this is that the novel
uses Shirley to idealise Moore. If she finds him so impressive
then so, presumably, should we. What happens, indeed, is a kind
of structural inversion of their roles. The 'social' character Moore
becomes a figure of chiefly sexual interest, while the 'sexual'
character Shirley ('sexual' on account of her passionate charismatic
presence) is projected into a public figure. There is an ideological
reason for this inversion. By 'sexualising' Moore, the novel to some
degree displaces his significance as social exploiter; and by con-
verting Shirley's exuberant personality into a social force, it partly
conceals the structural causes of Moore's capitalist cold-hearted-
ness by implying that what is at stake is a question of personal
temperament. Moreover, Shirley's stylish verve smooths and
buttresses Moore's position: she shares his social interests but
does with all the grace, fervour and flair he lacks, and so
renders them more palatable: 'I feel like Robert, only more fierily.'
Conflict in *Shirley* is displaced to Louis Moore, whose sexual
sadism intimates aspects of Charlotte's world less palpable in the
novel as a whole. The ferocious power-struggles of the other works,
focused as they are on the petty bourgeoise adrift as an internal
*émigré* in polite society, are here significantly sedated. The broad
confrontation between the ruling class and a notionally present
proletariat swallows up, or at least drastically defuses, those
crucial combats *within* respectable society which preoccupy the
other novels.

One result of this is a certain dislocation between Romance and
realism, subjectivity and society. It is, as we have seen, a common
disjunction in Charlotte Brontë; but in a novel like *Jane Eyre*,
Romantic aspiration and the real world engage in sharp dramatic
struggle as well as pulling dualistically apart. Because *Shirley* on
the whole evades such confrontations, containing them within the
private world of Caroline, it presents itself with a formal problem.
If *The Professor* reveals a rigorous suppression of subjectivity,
*Shirley* is remarkable for the maladroitness with which it tries to
synchronise its 'first' and third-person narrative levels, its interior
world and its social realism. One synchronising solution it explores
is that of myth: for myth injects unusual imaginative intensity

into a universe of concrete events. This, indeed, is precisely what *Shirley* aims to achieve: as the glorious legend of a heroic capitalist class it strives to conjure a Romantic myth out of real history, to create a mythology of bourgeois enterprise. Myth and realism intersect in the Carlylean image of the captain of industry; yet though myth is one way of spanning the gulf between imagination and social reality, the novel proves incapable of sustaining it. The public mythology it struggles to shape is too often diffused into weird private soliloquising, dissolved to an unstaunched gushing of lonely fantasy:

> 'It is not the daughter of Cadmus I see; nor do I realize her fatal longing to look on Jove in the majesty of his god-head. It is a priest of Juno that stands before me, watching late and lone at a shrine in an Argive temple. For years of solitary ministry, he has lived on dreams; there is divine madness upon him: he loves the idol he serves, and prays day and night that his frenzy may be fed, and that the Ox-eyed may smile on her votary. She has heard; she will be propitious. All Argos slumbers. The doors of the temple are shut: the priest waits at the altar.'[1]

It seems a far cry from the dyeing-vats. Far from providing the terms on which 'reality' may be negotiated, myths of this kind are mere interludes of imaginative relief, pockets of surplus emotion unabsorbed by the realist narrative. Thematically, myth and realism converge in the idealising conclusion; formally, the book is ripped apart between poetry and documentary.

One way of spotlighting this disjunction is to see *Shirley* as a sort of hybrid of two contemporary forms of 'social problem' novel, those of Disraeli and Mrs Gaskell. Disraeli's tactic in the *Coningsby* trilogy is to filter social experience through a garishly coloured, shamelessly ideological prism. That controlling ideology pares dashingly away at empirical detail, discovering a mirror-image of itself in the very pattern of social experience it has cunningly created. This allows Disraeli to achieve a 'totality' of sorts, but one so flagrantly imposed and tendentious that its cavalier remoteness from real conditions is blatant. Mrs Gaskell's empiricist liberalism, by contrast, allows her to explore those conditions while sapping her capacity to grasp the class-structure as a whole, limiting positive response to personal gesture and

fairy-tale gambit. *Shirley*, one might argue, is at once more
Romantic than Mrs Gaskell and more empiricist than Disraeli –
rather, perhaps, as Jane Eyre is both more spontaneous and more
cautious than St John Rivers. This is one reason why it is a difficult
novel to know how to read. On the one hand, *à la* Disraeli, it
dramatises a range of vivid 'mythical' types within a firmly
ideological ordering; on the other hand, it humbly disclaims any
programmatic intent, declaring itself modestly quotidian in style
and scope. If Caroline Helstone would slip unnoticed into a Mrs
Gaskell novel, Shirley would not be out of place in Disraeli. The
novel veers unsteadily between Romantic conservatism and progressive liberalism, bringing them finally to synthetic resolution:
in the end, Romantic imagery goes to consecrate a pragmatic
furthering of material interests. It is just that this thematic resolution is unable to reproduce itself at the level of literary form.

All Charlotte's novels, I would argue, reveal a dangerous 'residue'
of potentially uncontrollable emotion; and the success of a particular work depends in part on how effectively this is handled. I have
claimed in the case of *The Professor* that this emotion is over-
controlled, whereas in *Shirley* it is inadequately assimilated to the
realist narrative. Of course, the passionless objectivity of *The
Professor* is a paradoxical triumph of authorial subjectivity – the
achievement of a man whose control of the world is complete
enough to allow for coolness. In a parallel way, the descriptive
sections of *Shirley* are not wholly distinct in kind from the out-
bursts of private fantasy which stud them. In the apparently
neutral act of observation, the author betrays a private urge to
savage by caricature those who oppose her values: fat Dissenters,
mutinous workers, vulgar clerics. Robert Moore refrains from
hunting down his would-be assassin, but the novel steps in on
Moore's behalf and kills the fellow off with a bad dose of *delirium
tremens*.

The friction between 'realism' and 'imagination', then, manifests
itself not only as theme but also as a problem of how to write. It is
a dilemma structural to the Brontës' situation, as women brought
up in a disturbed social environment yet privately nourished on myth
and archetype; and that dichotomy reproduces itself as a stylistic
unevenness in the texts themselves. This, indeed, is one instance
of a duality common to the novels of the 1840s, where innovating

efforts to grapple directly with social experience fall back at points of ideological deadlock on to a ready-made lineage of literary devices. *Shirley* is a novel which confronts from the outset its own problematical character as a piece of fiction:

> If you think, from this prelude, that anything like a romance is preparing for you, reader, you were never more mistaken. Do you anticipate sentiment, and poetry, and reverie? Do you expect passion, stimulus, and melodrama? Calm your expectations; reduce them to a lowly standard. Something real, cool, and solid, lies before you; something unromantic as Monday morning, when all who have work wake with the consciousness that they must rise and betake themselves thereto.[2]

Passion, stimulus and melodrama are, in fact, embarrassingly abundant in *Shirley*, but the novel is from the start combatively prepared to deny the charge. Charlotte, it would seem, can produce a 'social problem' novel only by disowning her Romantic impulse with suspiciously emphatic forthrightness; and indeed the ideological assumption lurking behind this quotation, that 'social' novels inevitably move at a drably prosaic level, is itself Romantic enough. The fact is excused, as it were, by being defiantly brandished. We shall find as we read on that the book does in fact have regular recourse to 'poetical' gestures; there is a telling contrast between its inflated idealising of the ordinary and the Gateshead or Lowood scenes of *Jane Eyre*, where tenacious realism and fine imaginative force easily cohabit. But at the same time *Shirley* feels the need to be wary of its own mythologising: Mrs Pryor comments mildly at the end of one of Shirley's intoxicated reveries that it all seems 'rather fanciful', even though her comment is neatly timed so as not actually to cut short the extravaganza. At the end of the novel, 'imagination' is similarly interrogated by 'realism', but with a wry sense of futility:

> Are you not aware . . . that a discriminating public has its crochets: that the unvarnished truth does not answer: that plain facts will not digest? Do you not know that the squeak of the real pig is no more relished now than it was in days of yore? Were I to give the catastrophe of your life and conversation, the public would sweep off in shrieking hysterics, and

D

there would be a wild cry for sal-volatile and burnt feathers. 'Impossible!' would be pronounced here: 'untrue!' would be responded there. 'Inartistic!' would be solemnly decided. Note well! Whenever you present the actual, simple truth, it is, somehow, always denounced as a lie: they disown it, cast it off, throw it on the parish; whereas the product of your own imagination, the mere figment, the sheer fiction, is adopted, petted, termed pretty, proper, sweetly natural: the little spurious wretch gets all the comfits, – the honest, lawful banting, all the cuffs.[3]

The passage has it deftly both ways, celebrating the superiority of hard fact while regretting its implausibility, and so leaving a certain leeway for the dourly despised imagination.

*Villette* shows certain similar formal problems to *Shirley*; indeed, the disabling duality I have identified in the earlier novel is inscribed in the very trajectory of Lucy Snowe's career. We move from the cool, sententious Lucy of the Bretton household, preening herself on her spectatorial sang-froid, to the restless, heated, distraught governess in her drugged stumbling through the garish streets of Villette, enmeshed in a sinister Jesuit plot. Both images suggest a lop-sided balance of feeling and rationality, subject and object; we are as unconvinced by Lucy's over-protesting claims to rational calm at the beginning of the book as we are embarrassed by the paranoid fantasies of scheming Papists which end it. Whereas in *Shirley* enterprise and passivity were split into the respective roles of Shirley and Caroline, *Villette* tries like *Jane Eyre* to combine those functions within a single protagonist; and while this at least means dispensing with a merely glamorised figure, the combination is poorly achieved. The two aspects of Lucy interact locally, but they achieve no dialectical relation in the book as a whole. Instead, an initial phase of self-parodic 'realism' gives way with hardly a struggle before a swelling tide of inner tumult in which 'realism' is in the end effectively dissolved. A contrast with Jane Eyre may enforce the point. Jane is at various times both pettily malicious and impetuously emotional; but because her character is shaped within a complex dialectic of the analytic and the imaginative, she is rarely as *unreservedly* malicious or emotional as Lucy is. Lucy's spiteful characterisations of Belgians in general and her pupils in particular would be considerably too self-betraying in the mouth of the meek Jane Eyre. Her malice is, of course, the mental vengeance of the socially insecure, and so has the same root as her effusive emotionalism; but in the texture of writing it is the cleavage rather than the continuity between these two facets which is the more obtrusive. When Lucy speaks of how she controls her unruly pupils, her tones are clearly those of Crimsworth; it is the overt calculation here which would be inadmissable in *Jane Eyre*. But if Lucy is more calculating Crimsworthian than Jane, she is also more defence-lessly confessional in her emotional life. Once the mask of flagrantly synthetic *froideur* has slipped, Lucy lacks all edge and shield to her feelings. Her pose as icy observer is, as it were, confiscated by Madame Beck on her arrival in Villette; and once there is another character to fulfil this function, Lucy herself is partly redefined. Stripped of most of her defences, she is reduced to a Romantic victim:

> I did long, achingly, then and for four-and-twenty hours after-wards, for something to fetch me out of my present existence, and lead me upwards and onwards. This longing, and all of a similar kind, it was necessary to knock on the head; which I did, figuratively, after the manner of Jael to Sisera, driving a nail through their temples. Unlike Sisera, they did not die: they were but transiently stunned, and at intervals would turn on the nail with a rebellious wrench: then did the temples bleed, and the brain thrill to its core.[4]

And from here onwards the novel is studded with agonised soliloquies, tortuous self-lacerations, outpourings of spiritual wretchedness. One example may suffice:

> Between twelve and one that night a cup was forced to my lips, black, strong, strange, drawn from no well, but filled up seeth-ing from a bottomless and boundless sea. Suffering, brewed in temporal or calculable measure, and mixed for mortal lips, tastes not as this suffering tasted. . . . I rose on my knees in bed. Some fearful hours went over me: indescribably was I torn, racked and oppressed in mind. Amidst the horrors of that dream I think the worst lay here. Methought the well-loved dead, who had loved *me* well in life, met me elsewhere, alien-

ated; galled was my inmost spirit with an unutterable sense of
despair about the future.[5]

Similar though these passages are to the rhetorical flights of
*Shirley*, they differ in a notable quality – that of authenticity.
There is a marked contrast between the shoddily belletristic set-
pieces of *Shirley*, with their inexact flourishes and self-indulgent
'wonder', and the pressure of feeling which informs these alienated imaginings. What is equally striking, however, is the excess
of these feelings over their objects. In one sense, that excess is
the point: it is precisely in the disproportion of sensibility to
material situation, the imaginative surplus value, as it were, that
the measure of Lucy's victimisation can be taken. But there is a
contrast here with *Jane Eyre*. There are 'high' flights of feeling and
fancy in *Jane Eyre*, but these seem to some extent justified
by the 'high' drama of the narrative: a concealed madwoman,
a bigamously-minded aristocrat, a fanatical cleric. In this sense,
experience and event interact more or less successfully; passions
have their roughly adequate objects and motivations. There is
little in *Villette*, however, to motivate Lucy's emotional torment.
Whereas in *Jane Eyre* imaginative intimations are confirmed by
fact – there *is* a frightful mystery at Thornfield – the reverse is
true of *Villette*: the absurd nun turns out to be a mere cover for
schoolgirl flirtation. 'Real' life is tame enough – at any rate until
the very end of the novel, when the conspiracy is sprung upon us.
But the hollowness of this merely proves how inept the novel is
when it tries to ratify its heroine's responses by demonstrating
the world to be objectively sinister. Charlotte Brontë once referred
to Lucy's inner life as partly 'morbid'; but while this is clear
enough to the reader, it is far from obvious that it is clear to the
novel. The book seems unable to establish an operative distance
between itself and its heroine – unable to steer between the forced
repression and uncontrolled release of feeling.

In *Villette*, as in *Shirley*, the act of writing becomes itself
problematical. The novel has a *Shirley*-like uncertainty about what
kind of work it intends itself to be, as its similar gambit of un-
leashing and then undercutting Romantic outpourings shows.
This happens with its treatment of the ghostly nun, and it crops up
too when Lucy is crossing the Channel to Europe:

In my reverie, methought I saw the continent of Europe, like a
wide dream-land, far away. Sunshine lay on it, making the long
coast one line of gold; tiniest tracery of clustered town and
snow-gleaming tower, of woods deep massed, of heights serrated,
of smooth pasturage and veiny stream embossed the metal-
bright prospect. . . .
   Cancel the whole of that, if you please, reader – or rather let
it stand, and draw thence a moral – an alliterative, text-hand
copy –
           *'Day-dreams are delusions of the demon.'*
Becoming excessively sick, I faltered down into the cabin.[6]

But the chief locus of this hesitation is surely the novel's ending:
the deliberate ambiguity as to whether Paul dies at sea or not:

That storm roared frenzied for seven days. It did not cease till
the Atlantic was strewn with wrecks; it did not lull till the
deeps had gorged their full of sustenance. Not till the destroying
angel of tempest had achieved his perfect work, would he fold
the wings whose waft was thunder – the tremor of whose plumes
was storm. . . .
   Here pause; pause at once. There is enough said. Trouble no
quiet, kind heart; leave sunny imaginations hope. Let it be
theirs to conceive the delight of joy born again fresh out of
great terror, the rapture of rescue from peril, the wondrous
reprieve from dread, the fruition of return. Let them picture
union and a happy succeeding life.[7]

Charlotte has habitually used the very forms of her fiction to
resolve stalemates in 'real' experience. The fairy-tale ending, the
lost parent, the sudden legacy, the timely coincidence – all these
fictional devices have been exploited to smooth the rough edges of
a history which seemed unlikely to pull through by its own internal
logic. But the device could operate only if it appeared innocent of
itself – if it, so to speak, naturalised itself, offered itself as a
component of content rather than a stratagem of form. The fact
that Charlotte tends in puritan fashion to conceive of 'real life'
biography as plot and fable assists that 'naturalising': she speaks,
with reference to Caroline Helstone, of 'the true narrative of life',
and thinks of the morally virtuous as heroes and heroines in life's

drama. But the ending of *Villette*, with its sudden alienation-effect, destroys at a stroke that innocence, that pretence of a fiction un- conscious of its own fictionality. Instead, fiction and fact are offered as alternatives, the veil stripped from the novelistic pose. Yet fiction is exposed for what it is only to be endorsed, relied on, reinstated: the novel has recourse to its own fictional status in order to half-evade the outcome threatened by its 'real' subject- matter. One might read this as an ironical *underscoring* of 'realism', detecting a note of suppressed puritan scorn for the anodyne imagination which sugars unsavoury facts. 'Sunny imaginations' might indeed prompt such a reading; for 'sunny' is associated in this novel with the Brettons' life-style, and so evokes the secret reservations which Lucy has felt about it. The imagination in *Villette* is on the side not of sunniness but of catastrophe and despair; so it is odd, almost oxymoronic, to find this phrase in the penultimate paragraph. We clearly *are* meant to sense, beneath the pious appeal to fancy, the paucity of such a tactic; yet on the other hand the impulse not to trouble the reader with tragedy – to succour rather than disturb, affirm rather than subvert – is a typical constituent of Charlotte's ideology. The ending, then, half- suppresses tragedy while simultaneously protesting against such a manoeuvre. It confesses the emptiness of the tactic while emotionally investing in it, displaying both the falsehood and pro- priety, the urgency and impotence, of the move it makes.

The three novels I have discussed so far reveal formal flaws which spring from a maladjustment between subject and object highly relevant to their subject-matter. It is here that *Jane Eyre* has the edge over them. *Jane Eyre* achieves, sporadically but sufficiently, what *Wuthering Heights* sustains throughout: an intense imaginative pressure which sharpens rather than dissi- pates a sense of the actual. For much of the novel, Jane's Romantic subjectivism is laced with stringent rationality, but it is not thereby pressed (as with Crimsworth or the early Lucy) almost to vanishing-point. She *is* at times rendered effectively invisible, personally nullified by a predatory society; but because of a subtle form of double focusing this invisibility is neither mere personal blankness (Crimsworth) nor an outer husk against which anarchic inner passion helplessly presses (Lucy). Jane lucidly observes others in the very act of hypersensitively checking their responses to her;

her rancorous protest against the way others objectify her contains an ironic consciousness of herself as an object in their eyes. This is so, for example, when she is put on show before the Lowood classroom: plunged into shame as she is, she and the novel are still *observing* Brocklehurst with outgoing dramatic objectivity. He exists as brutally autonomous, not merely as a blurred figment of the heroine's troubled mind. Personally negated though Jane is by much of the history she lives through, it is still the case that she 'lives' as a character in terms of her relation to a dramatic narrative. Her inner life is manifested to us situationally as much as confessionally; she is neither a purely private figure inhabiting a domain divorced from social reality, nor a merely behaviourist function of her social environment. In this sense she differs from Charlotte's other protagonists. Lucy's interior world is partly severed from the 'objective' narrative, sealed and guarded in a realm of quiet desperation; Caroline Helstone's spiritual biography is only loosely tied to a dramatic action which seems to move at a different fictional level. William Crimsworth, by contrast, after a preliminary conflict between poetic sensitivity and material pressure, comes to exist so completely in terms of his social achievement that he seems at points hardly more than a passive function of it.

*Jane Eyre*, however, reveals a more complex relation between individual and society; the heroine is for the most part neither as morbidly introspective as Lucy nor as coolly externalised as Crimsworth. The tension between 'Romance' and 'realism' is more deftly managed than elsewhere, as a contrast between Jane's flight from Thornfield and Lucy's dazed wanderings through Villette makes clear. Both scenes portray a grievous alienation; but whereas in *Villette* the overheated imagination warps and unhinges 'objective' reality, *Jane Eyre* gives us a brilliantly realised study of an alienated consciousness which remains nervously alert to actual events and places. When Rochester defines Jane as 'Romantic' in his whimsical talk of elves and sprites, Jane assumes a briskly disillusioning attitude; when Blanche Ingram dismisses her as insipid, Jane's secret spiritual resources tell her how wrong Blanche is. A contrast between Jane and Lucy may again illustrate the point. Lucy feels in the end paranoically oppressed by a whole society, epitomised by Madame Beck and her

cronies; she is reduced to an almost complete outsider, with only
Paul as a lifeline. But she is after all a literal alien in Villette,
whereas Jane, who is at once hot-headed rebel and genteel
governess, has a more intricate relationship with her society
which makes for more subtle emotional control. Since she is a
social rather than a literal stranger, the issues at stake are less
easily simplified to a chauvinistic contrast between English rectitude and European intrigue. (William Crimsworth also confronts
a literally foreign society, but this only goes to show how easily
English sang-froid and puritan perseverance can get the better
of it.) Jane is a social exile in comparison with Rochester, but it
is she who is 'inside', upholding the social code, when he proposes
bigamy.

It seems to me true that Charlotte Brontë's novels display a
roughly triadic structure if they are taken 'horizontally' as well as
'vertically' – true, that is to say, of the way their narratives are
periodised. Each novel is more or less trichotomised into a preliminary phase of domestic settlement, a break to isolation and
independence, and a final integration. To some extent the 'hori-
zontal' structure reflects the 'vertical' one, since each phase
corresponds broadly to one of the three main structural roles. Very
generally, the preliminary settlement corresponds to the function
of conservative authority, the transitional period of independence
belongs to the protagonist, and the concluding integration is with
the 'Romantic-radical' figure. Each work, however, shows a different distribution of emphasis between the three phases, and that
pattern reflects an ideological variation. In both later novels, for
example, the initial phase is considerably less oppressive than in
the first two. Caroline is hemmed in by an autocratic guardian, but
despite his name Helstone is not unsympathetically presented;
Lucy Snowe's situation is formally parallel to Jane's, but she is
a good deal happier than Jane and at least has (curiously invisible)
kin of her own. The novel in fact slides over the question of Lucy's
relations with her immediate family: whether she is happy or
not with them is left deliberately ambiguous, and the catastrophe
which overtakes them rendered obscurely metaphorical. The point
of this is to pitch Lucy into Jane's position of sturdy self-reliance
without having to oppose anybody in the process. Lucy effects no
rebellious break with either her own family or the Brettons: it is

simply that the Bretton fortunes melt away and force her out in the world. The novel's avoidance of confrontation at this point is in keeping with its general swaddling of social conflict.

It is evident that the triple phasing I have described applies less to *Shirley* than to the other novels. In *Shirley*, indeed, the crucial 'break' remains unacted: Caroline does not realise her plans to leave home and attains instead to a vicarious self-fulfilment through Shirley, one which allows her to remain where she is. The 'break' is displaced to a question of consciousness; and this, as I have argued, is symptomatic of the novel's drive towards harmony rather than dissonance. Roughly the reverse is true of Crimsworth's case: with him, the break (a double rupture, in fact, first from his relations and then from Edward) is swift, clean and simple, costing the minimum of emotional expenditure. This suits the novel's ideological slant: since its focus rests firmly on progress and enterprise, inherited bonds and sentiments may be briskly disowned.

What distinguishes *Jane Eyre*, however, is that the primordial moment of embracing one's lonely destiny is neither muffled, displaced, nor efficiently dispatched. Jane's showdown with Mrs Reed is a grippingly dramatic encounter, in which Mrs Reed's reactions as well as Jane's are subjected to intensely detailed scrutiny. Beside it, Crimsworth's rejection of Edward seems considerably too angled and subjective an account, too confidently in Crimsworth's iron control.

*Jane Eyre* differs too in that it has four rather than three phases – or rather, that its second phase is divided between Rochester and St John Rivers. A comparison of Rivers with other authoritarians in the novels suggests one reason for *Jane Eyre*'s aesthetic superiority. Almost all the conservative autocrats (Reuter, Rivers, Helstone, Beck) are qualifiedly admired; the only major exception is Edward Crimsworth, who is as charmless as the novel he inhabits. But despite the combination of liberal distaste and imaginative sympathy with which they are portrayed, none of them is as effectively complex a character as Rivers. It is a mark of the novel's distinction that its autocrat is neither a straw target like Mdlle Reuter, a one-dimensional oppressor like Edward Crimsworth, a Tory stereotype like Helstone, a furtive Romantic like Moore or a cluster of inconsistencies like Madame Beck. Rivers is an absorb-

D*

ingly complicated figure, in no sense a mere symbol. In *The Professor* and *Shirley*, much of the autocrat's energy is shifted on to the 'Romantic' type – Hunsden and Shirley – who by uniting dominance with glamour effectively confiscates the autocrat's role. Rivers, however, has a formidable life of his own, and himself appropriates some of Rochester's Romantic passion. It is, indeed, a sign of *Jane Eyre's* imaginative stamina that at the end of the Rochester débâcle, when the novel appears to have spent itself in cathartic crisis, it retains the energy to move into a quite new phase.

I have tried in this chapter to outline some significant relations between categorial structure, literary form and aesthetic value in Charlotte Brontë's fiction. From the heart of specific historical pressures, a dominant structure of consciousness crystallises out – an uneven and ambiguous one, sure enough, combining disparate elements into conflictive unity, but identifiable none the less by the recurrence of certain set relations in the fiction. This ideological structure, which is the very form of the author's imagination, marks out a field of possible literary forms. I have tried to show how the novels weave variations on a consistent 'deep' structure, in an attempt to resolve that structure's internal contradictions. The extent to which those contradictions are reproduced in certain limits and failures of literary form seems to me a crucial factor in determining the question of aesthetic value. It is with these considerations in mind that we may turn to *Wuthering Heights*.

# 6 *Wuthering Heights*

If it is a function of ideology to achieve an illusory resolution of real contradictions, then Charlotte Brontë's novels are ideological in a precise sense – myths. In the fabulous, fairy-tale ambience of a work like *Jane Eyre*, with its dramatic archetypes and magical devices, certain facets of the complex mythology which constitutes Victorian bourgeois consciousness find their aesthetically appropriate form. Yet 'myth' is, of course, a term more commonly used of *Wuthering Heights*; and we need therefore to discriminate between different meanings of the word.

For Lucien Goldmann, 'ideology' in literature is to be sharply distinguished from what he terms 'world-view'. Ideology signifies a false, distortive, partial consciousness; 'world-view' designates a true, total and coherent understanding of social relations. This seems to me a highly suspect formulation: nothing, surely, could be more ideological than the 'tragic vision' of Pascal and Racine which Goldmann examines in *The Hidden God*. Even so, Goldmann's questionable distinction can be used to illuminate a crucial difference between the work of Charlotte and Emily Brontë. Charlotte's fiction is 'mythical' in the exact ideological sense I have suggested: it welds together antagonistic forces, forging from them a pragmatic, precarious coherence of interests. *Wuthering Heights* is mythical in a more traditional sense of the term: an apparently timeless, highly integrated, mysteriously autonomous symbolic universe. Such a notion of myth is itself, of course, ideologically based, and much of this chapter will be an attempt to de-mystify it. The world of *Wuthering Heights* is neither eternal nor self-enclosed; nor is it in the least unriven by internal contradictions. But in the case of this work it does seem necessary to speak of a 'world-view', a unified vision of brilliant clarity and consistency, in contrast to the dominant consciousness of Charlotte's novels. Goldmann's distinction is valuable to that limited extent: it enforces an appropriate contrast between the elaborated impersonality of Emily's novel, the 'intensive totality' of its world,[1] and Charlotte's tendentious, occasionally opportunist manipulation of materials for ideological ends, her readiness to allow a set of practical interests to predominate over the demands of disinterested exploration. If *Wuthering Heights* generally transcends those limits, it is not in the least because its universe is any less ideological, or that conflictive pressures are absent from it. The difference lies in the paradoxical truth that *Wuthering Heights* achieves its coherence of vision from an exhausting confrontation of contending forces, whereas Charlotte's kind of totality depends upon a pragmatic integration of them. Both forms of consciousness are ideological; but in so far as Emily's represents a more penetrative, radical and honest enterprise, it provides the basis for a finer artistic achievement. *Wuthering Heights* remains formally unfissured by the conflicts it dramatises; it forges its unity of vision from the very imaginative heat those conflicts generate. The book's genealogical structure is relevant here: familial relations at once provide the substance of antagonism and mould that substance into intricate shape, precipitating a tightly integrated form from the very stuff of struggle and disintegration. The genealogical structure, moreover, allows for a sharply dialectical relation between the 'personal' and 'impersonal' of a sort rare in Charlotte: the family, at once social institution and domain of intensely interpersonal relationships, highlights the complex interplay between an evolving system of given unalterable relations and the creation of individual value.

One is tempted, then, to credit Goldmann's dubious dichotomy between ideology and world-view to this extent: that if 'ideology' is a coherence of antagonisms, 'world-view' is a coherent perception of them.* An instance of such coherent perception may be found in Emily Brontë's early essay, 'The Butterfly':

All creation is equally insane. There are those flies playing above the stream, swallows and fish diminishing their number

---

* A coherence which is partial, limited, defined as much by its absences and exclusions as by its affirmations, and so (*pace* Goldmann) ideological.

each minute: these will become in their turn, the prey of some tyrant of air or water; and man for his amusement or his needs will kill their murderers. Nature is an inexplicable puzzle, life exists on a principle of destruction; every creature must be the relentless instrument of death to the others, or himself cease to live.[2]

This, clearly enough, is ideological to the point of prefiguring Social Darwinism; but it is difficult to imagine Charlotte having written with this degree of generalising impersonal poise, this fluent projection of fearful private vision into total, lucid statement. Charlotte, indeed, seems to have recognised something of this difference with her sister. 'In some points', she once wrote, 'I consider Emily somewhat of a theorist; now and then she broaches ideas which strike my sense as much more daring and original than practical.'[3] Defining the issue as a contrast between theory and practice seems significant: the cautious empiricist greets the totalising visionary with a mixture of respect and reservation. It certainly seems true of Charlotte that her *imaginative* daring is not coupled with any equivalent moral or intellectual boldness. Hunsden, Rochester, Shirley, Paul Emmanuel: all combine a civilised moderation with their Romantic radicalism, which could hardly be said of Heathcliff. Heathcliff, as Lockwood finds to his cost, is precisely *not* a rough diamond; he conceals no coy Hunsden-like affection beneath his barbarous behaviour.

The difference between Charlotte and Emily can be expressed another way. The spite, violence and bigotry which in *Wuthering Heights* are aspects of the narrative are in parts of Charlotte's fiction qualities of the narration. *Wuthering Heights* trades in spite and stiff-neckedness, but always 'objectively', as the power of its tenaciously detailed realism to survive unruffled even the gustiest of emotional crises would suggest. Malice and narrowness in Charlotte's work, by contrast, are occasionally authorial as well as thematic, so that characters and events are flushed with the novelist's ideological intentions, bear the imprint of her longings and anxieties. This, as I have argued, is less true of *Jane Eyre*, where a subtler epistomology grants the objective world its own relative solidity: we feel the menacingly autonomous existence of Brocklehurst, Mrs Reed, even Bertha, as we do not with Père Silas,

Madame Walravens or Job Barraclough. Because these figures are so directly the spontaneous precipitates of authorial fantasy, they have both the vividness and the vacuity of Lucy Snowe's dazed perceptions. We are almost never at a loss what to think about a Charlotte character, which could hardly be said of *Wuthering Heights*. No mere critical hair-splitting can account for the protracted debate over whether Heathcliff is hero or demon, Catherine tragic heroine or spoilt brat, Nelly Dean shrewd or stupid. The narrative techniques of the novel are deliberately framed to preserve these ambivalences; those of Charlotte Brontë allow us fairly direct access to a single, transparent, controlling consciousness which maintains its dominance even when its bearer is in practice subdued and subordinated.

I have said that *Wuthering Heights* remains unriven by the conflicts it releases, and it contrasts as such with those Charlotte works which are formally flawed by the strains and frictions of their 'content'. Charlotte's fiction sets out to reconcile thematically what I have crudely termed 'Romance' and 'realism' but sometimes displays severe structural disjunctions between the two; *Wuthering Heights* fastens thematically on a near-absolute antagonism between these modes but achieves, structurally and stylistically, an astonishing unity between them. Single incidents are inseparably high drama and domestic farce, figures like Catherine Earnshaw contradictory amalgams of the passionate and the pettish. There seems to me an ideological basis to this paradoxical contrast between the two sisters' works. Charlotte's novels, as I have suggested, are ideological in that they exploit fiction and fable to smooth the jagged edges of real conflict, and the evasions which that entails emerge as aesthetic unevennesses – as slanting, overemphasis, idealisation, structural dissonance. *Wuthering Heights*, on the other hand, confronts the tragic truth that the passion and society it presents are not fundamentally reconcilable – that there remains at the deepest level an ineradicable contradiction between them which refuses to be unlocked, which obtrudes itself as the very stuff and secret of experience. It is, then, precisely the imagination capable of confronting this tragic duality which has the power to produce the aesthetically superior work – which can synchronise in its internal structures the most shattering passion with the most rigorous realist control. The more authentic social and moral recognitions of the book, in other words, generate a finer artistic control; the unflinchingness with which the novel penetrates into fundamental contradictions is realised in a range of richer imaginative perceptions.

The primary contradiction I have in mind is the choice posed for Catherine between Heathcliff and Edgar Linton. That choice seems to me the pivotal event of the novel, the decisive catalyst of the tragedy; and if this is so, then the crux of *Wuthering Heights* must be conceded by even the most remorselessly mythological and mystical of critics to be a social one. In a crucial act of self-betrayal and bad faith, Catherine rejects Heathcliff as a suitor because he is socially inferior to Linton; and it is from this that the train of destruction follows. Heathcliff's own view of the option is not, of course, to be wholly credited: he is clearly wrong to think that Edgar 'is scarcely a degree dearer [to Catherine] than her dog, or her horse'.[4] Linton lacks spirit, but he is, as Nelly says, kind, honourable and trustful, a loving husband to Catherine and utterly distraught at her loss. Even so, the perverse act of *mauvaise foi* by which Catherine trades her authentic selfhood for social privilege is rightly denounced by Heathcliff as spiritual suicide and murder:

> '*Why* did you betray your own heart, Cathy? I have not one word of comfort. You deserve this. You have killed yourself. Yes, you may kiss me, and cry; and ring out my kisses and tears: they'll blight you – they'll damn you. You loved me – then what *right* had you to leave me? What right – answer me – for the poor fancy you felt for Linton? Because misery and degradation, and death, and nothing that God or Satan could inflict would have parted us, *you*, of your own will, did it. I have not broken your heart – *you* have broken it; and in breaking it, you have broken mine.'[5]

Like Lucy Snowe, Catherine tries to lead two lives: she hopes to square authenticity with social convention, running in harness an ontological commitment to Heathcliff with a phenomenal relationship to Linton. 'I *am* Heathcliff!' is dramatically arresting, but it is also a way of keeping the outcast at arm's length, evading the challenge he offers. If Catherine is Heathcliff – if identity rather than relationship is in question – then their estrangement is inconceivable, and Catherine can therefore turn to others without violating the timeless metaphysical idea Heathcliff embodies. She finds in him an integrity of being denied or diluted in routine social relations; but to preserve that ideal means reifying him to a Hegelian essence, sublimely untainted by empirical fact. Heathcliff, understandably, refuses to settle for this: he would rather enact his essence in existence by becoming Catherine's lover. He can, it seems, be endowed with impressive ontological status only at the price of being nullified as a person.

The uneasy alliance of social conformity and personal fulfilment for which Charlotte's novels works is not, then, feasible in the world of *Wuthering Heights*; Catherine's attempt to compromise unleashes the contradictions which will drive both her and Heathcliff to their deaths. One such contradiction lies in the relation between Heathcliff and the Earnshaw family. As a waif and orphan, Heathcliff is inserted into the close-knit family structure as an alien; he emerges from that ambivalent domain of darkness which is the 'outside' of the tightly defined domestic system. That darkness is ambivalent because it is at once fearful and fertilising, as Heathcliff himself is both gift and threat. Earnshaw's first words about him make this clear: ' "See here, wife! I was never so beaten with anything in my life: but you must e'en take it as a gift of God; though it's as dark almost as if it came from the devil." '[6] Stripped as he is of determinate social relations, of a given function within the family, Heathcliff's presence is radically gratuitous; the arbitrary, unmotivated event of his arrival at the Heights offers its inhabitants a chance to transcend the constrictions of their self-enclosed social structure and gather him in. Because Heathcliff's circumstances are so obscure he is available to be accepted or rejected simply for himself, laying claim to no status other than a human one. He is, of course, proletarian in appearance, but the obscurity of his origins also frees him of any exact social role; as Nelly Dean muses later, he might equally be a prince. He is ushered into the Heights for no good reason other than to be arbitrarily loved; and in this sense he is a touchstone of others' responses, a liberating force for Cathy and a stumbling-block for others. Nelly hates him at first, unable to transcend her bigotry against the new and non-related; she puts him on the landing like a dog, hoping he will be gone by morning. Earnshaw pets and favours him, and in doing so creates fresh inequalities in the family hierarchy which become the source of Hindley's hatred. As heir to the Heights, Hindley understandably feels his social role subverted by this irrational, unpredictable intrusion.

Catherine, who does not expect to inherit, responds spontaneously to Heathcliff's presence; and because this antagonises Hindley she becomes after Earnshaw's death a spiritual orphan as Heathcliff is a literal one. Both are allowed to run wild; both become the 'outside' of the domestic structure. Because his birth is unknown, Heathcliff is a purely atomised individual, free of generational ties in a novel where genealogical relations are of crucial thematic and structural importance; and it is because he is an internal *émigré* within the Heights that he can lay claim to a relationship of direct personal equality with Catherine who, as the daughter of the family, is the least economically integral member. Heathcliff offers Catherine a friendship which opens fresh possibilities of freedom within the internal system of the Heights; in a situation where social determinants are insistent, freedom can mean only a relative independence of given blood-ties, of the settled, evolving, predictable structures of kinship. Whereas in Charlotte's fiction the severing or lapsing of such relations frees you for progress up the class-system, the freedom which Cathy achieves with Heathcliff takes her down that system, into consorting with a 'gypsy'. Yet 'down' is also 'outside', just as gypsy signifies 'lower class' but also asocial vagrant, classless natural life-form. As the eternal rocks beneath the woods, Heathcliff is both lowly and natural, enjoying the partial freedom from social pressures appropriate to those at the bottom of the class-structure. In loving Heathcliff, Catherine is taken outside the family and society into an opposing realm which can be adequately imaged only as 'Nature'.

The loving equality between Catherine and Heathcliff stands, then, as a paradigm of human possibilities which reach beyond, and might ideally unlock, the tightly dominative system of the Heights. Yet at the same time Heathcliff's mere presence fiercely intensifies that system's harshness, twisting all the Earnshaw relationships into bitter antagonism. He unwittingly sharpens a violence endemic to the Heights – a violence which springs both from the hard exigencies imposed by its struggle with the land, and from its social exclusiveness as a self-consciously ancient, respectable family. The violence which Heathcliff unwittingly triggers is turned against him: he is cast out by Hindley, culturally deprived, reduced to the status of farm-labourer. What Hindley does, in fact, is to invert the potential freedom symbolised by Heathcliff into a parody of itself, into the non-freedom of neglect. Heathcliff is robbed of liberty in two antithetical ways: exploited as a servant on the one hand, allowed to run wild on the other; and this contradiction is appropriate to childhood, which is a time of relative freedom from convention and yet, paradoxically, a phase of authoritarian repression. In this sense there is freedom for Heathcliff neither within society nor outside it; his two conditions are inverted mirror-images of one another. It is a contradiction which encapsulates a crucial truth about bourgeois society. If there is no genuine liberty on its 'inside' – Heathcliff is oppressed by work and the familial structure – neither is there more than a caricature of liberty on the 'outside', since the release of running wild is merely a function of cultural impoverishment. The friendship of Heathcliff and Cathy crystallises under the pressures of economic and cultural violence, so that the freedom it seems to signify ('half-savage and hardy, and free'') is always the other face of oppression, always exists in its shadow. With Heathcliff and Catherine, as in Charlotte's fiction, bitter social reality breeds Romantic escapism; but whereas Charlotte's novels try to trim the balance between them, *Wuthering Heights* shows a more dialectical interrelation at work. Romantic intensity is locked in combat with society, but cannot wholly transcend it; your freedom is bred and deformed in the shadow of your oppression, just as, in the adult Heathcliff, oppression is the logical consequence of the exploiter's 'freedom'.

Just as Hindley withdraws culture from Heathcliff as a mode of domination, so Heathcliff acquires culture as a weapon. He amasses a certain amount of cultural capital in his two years' absence in order to shackle others more effectively, buying up the expensive commodity of gentility in order punitively to re-enter the society from which he was punitively expelled. This is liberty of a kind, in contrast with his previous condition; but the novel is insistent on its ultimately illusory nature. In oppressing others the exploiter imprisons himself; the adult Heathcliff's systematic tormenting is fed by his victims' pain but also drains him of blood, impels and possesses him as an external force. His alienation from Catherine estranges him from himself to the point where his brutalities become tediously perfunctory gestures, the mechanical motions of a man who is already withdrawing himself from his own body. Heathcliff moves from being Hindley's victim to becoming, like Catherine, his own executioner.

Throughout *Wuthering Heights*, labour and culture, bondage and freedom, Nature and artifice appear at once as each other's dialectical negations and as subtly matched, mutually reflective. Culture – gentility – is the opposite of labour for young Heathcliff and Hareton; but it is also a crucial economic weapon, as well as a product of work itself. The delicate spiritless Lintons in their crimson-carpeted drawing-room are radically severed from the labour which sustains them; gentility grows from the production of others, detaches itself from that work (as the Grange is separate from the Heights), and then comes to dominate the labour on which it is parasitic. In doing so, it becomes a form of self-bondage; if work is servitude, so in a subtler sense is civilisation. To some extent, these polarities are held together in the yeoman-farming structure of the Heights. Here labour and culture, freedom and necessity, Nature and society are roughly complementary. The Earnshaws are gentlemen yet they work the land; they enjoy the freedom of being their own masters, but that freedom moves within the tough discipline of labour; and because the social unit of the Heights – the family – is both 'natural' (biological) and an economic system, it acts to some degree as a mediation between Nature and artifice, naturalising property relations and socialising blood-ties. Relationships in this isolated world are turbulently face-to-face, but they are also impersonally mediated through a working relation with Nature. This is not to share Mrs Q. D. Leavis's view of the Heights as 'a wholesome primitive and natural unit of a healthy society';[8] there does not, for instance, seem much that is wholesome about Joseph. Joseph incarnates a grimness inherent in conditions of economic exigency, where relationships must be tightly ordered and are easily warped into violence. One of *Wuthering Heights*' more notable achievements is ruthlessly to de-mystify the Victorian notion of the family as a pious, pacific

space within social conflict. Even so, the Heights does pin together contradictions which the entry of Heathcliff will break
open. Heathcliff disturbs the Heights because he is simply superfluous: he has no defined place within its biological and economic
system. (He may well be Catherine's illegitimate half-brother, just
as he may well have passed his two-year absence in Tunbridge
Wells.) The superfluity he embodies is that of a sheerly human
demand for recognition; but since there is no space for such surplus
within the terse economy of the Heights, it proves destructive
rather than creative in effect, straining and overloading already
taut relationships. Heathcliff catalyses an aggression intrinsic to
Heights society; that sound blow Hindley hands out to Catherine
on the evening of Heathcliff's first appearance is slight but significant evidence against the case that conflict starts only with Heathcliff's arrival.

The effect of Heathcliff is to explode those conflicts into antagonisms which finally rip the place apart. In particular, he marks
the beginnings of that process whereby passion and personal intensity separate out from the social domain and offer an alternative
commitment to it. For farming families like the Earnshaws, work
and human relations are roughly coterminous: work is socialised,
personal relations mediated through a context of labour. Heathcliff, however, is set to work meaninglessly, as a servant rather
than a member of the family; and his fervent emotional life with
Catherine is thus forced outside the working environment into
the wild Nature of the heath, rather than Nature reclaimed and
worked up into significant value in the social activity of labour.
Heathcliff is stripped of culture in the sense of gentility, but the
result is a paradoxical intensifying of his fertile imaginative liaison
with Catherine. It is fitting, then, that their free, neglected
wanderings lead them to their adventure at Thrushcross Grange.
For if the Romantic childhood culture of Catherine and Heathcliff
exists in a social limbo divorced from the minatory world of
working relations, the same can be said in a different sense of the
genteel culture of the Lintons, surviving as it does on the basis of
material conditions it simultaneously conceals. As the children
spy on the Linton family, that concealed brutality is unleashed in
the shape of bulldogs brought to the defence of civility. The
natural energy in which the Linton's culture is rooted bursts liter-

ally through to savage the 'savages' who appear to threaten
property. The underlying truth of violence, continuously visible
at the Heights, is momentarily exposed; old Linton thinks the
intruders are after his rents. Culture draws a veil over such brute
force but also sharpens it: the more property you have, the more
ruthlessly you need to defend it. Indeed, Heathcliff himself seems
dimly aware of how cultivation exacerbates 'natural' conflict, as
we see in his scornful account of the Linton children's petulant
squabbling; cultivation, by pampering and swaddling 'natural'
drives, at once represses serious physical violence and breeds a
neurasthenic sensitivity which allows selfish impulse free rein.
'Natural' aggression is nurtured both by an excess and an
absence of culture – a paradox demonstrated by Catherine Earnshaw, who is at once wild and pettish, savage and spoilt. Nature
and culture, then, are locked in a complex relation of antagonism
and affinity: the Romantic fantasies of Heathcliff and Catherine,
and the Romantic Linton drawing-room with its gold-bordered
ceiling and shimmering chandelier, both bear the scars of the
material conditions which produced them – scars visibly inscribed
on Cathy's ankle. Yet to leave the matter there would be to draw
a purely formal parallel. For what distinguishes the two forms of
Romance is Heathcliff: his intense communion with Catherine is
an uncompromising rejection of the Linton world.

The opposition, however, is not merely one between the values
of personal relationship and those of conventional society. What
prevents this is the curious impersonality of the relationship between Catherine and Heathcliff. Edgar Linton shows at his best a
genuine capacity for tender, loving fidelity; but this thrives on
obvious limits. The limits are those of the closed room into which
the children peer – the glowing, sheltered space within which those
close, immediate encounters which make for both tenderness and
pettishness may be conducted. Linton is released from material
pressures into such a civilised enclave; and in that sense his situation differs from that of the Heights, where personal relations
are more intimately entwined with a working context. The relationship of Heathcliff and Catherine, however, provides a third
term. It really is a personal relationship, yet seems also to transcend the personal into some region beyond it. Indeed, there is a
sense in which the unity the couple briefly achieve is narrowed

and degutted by being described as 'personal'. In so far as
'personal' suggests the liberal humanism of Edgar, with his
concern (crudely despised by Heathcliff) for pity, charity and
humanity, the word is clearly inapplicable to the fierce mutual
tearings of Catherine and Heathcliff. Yet it is inadequate to the
positive as well as the destructive aspects of their love. Their
relationship is, we say, 'ontological' or 'metaphysical' because it
opens out into the more-than-personal, enacts a style of being
which is more than just the property of two individuals, which
suggests in its impersonality something beyond a merely Romantic-
individualist response to social oppression. Their relationship
articulates a depth inexpressible in routine social practice, transcendent of available social languages. Its impersonality suggests
both a savage depersonalising and a paradigmatic significance; and
in neither sense is the relationship wholly within their conscious
control. What Heathcliff offers Cathy is a non- or pre-social
relationship, as the only authentic form of living in a world of
exploitation and inequality, a world where one must refuse to
measure oneself by the criteria of the class-structure and so must
appear inevitably subversive. Whereas in Charlotte's novels the
love-relationship takes you into society, in *Wuthering Heights*
it drives you out of it. The love between Heathcliff and Catherine
is an intuitive intimacy raised to cosmic status, by-passing the
mediation of the 'social'; and this, indeed, is both its strength and
its limit. Its non-sociality is on the one hand a revolutionary
refusal of the given language of social roles and values; and if the
relationship is to remain unabsorbed by society it must therefore
appear as natural rather than social, since Nature is the 'outside'
of society. On the other hand, the novel cannot realise the meaning of that revolutionary refusal in social terms; the most it can
do is to *universalise* that meaning by intimating the mysteriously
impersonal energies from which the relationship springs.

   Catherine, of course, *is* absorbed: she enters the civilised world
of the Lintons and leaves Heathcliff behind, to become a 'wolfish,
pitiless' man. To avoid incorporation means remaining as un-
reclaimed as the wild furze: there is no way in this novel of
temporising between conformity and rebellion. But there is
equally no way for the revolutionary depth of relationship between Heathcliff and Catherine to realise itself as a historical

force; instead, it becomes an elusive dream of absolute value, an incomparably more powerful version of Charlotte's myth of lost origins. Catherine and Heathcliff seek to preserve the primordial moment of pre-social harmony, before the fall into history and oppression. But it won't do to see them merely as children eternally fixated in some Edenic infancy: we do not see them merely as children, and in any case to be 'merely' a child is to endure the punitive pressures of an adult world. Moreover, it is none of Heathcliff's fault that the relationship remains 'metaphysical': it is Catherine who consigns it to unfulfilment. Their love remains an unhistorical essence which fails to enter into concrete existence and can do so, ironically, only in death. Death, indeed, as the ultimate outer limit of consciousness and society, is the locus of Catherine and Heathcliff's love, the horizon on which it moves. The absolutism of death is prefigured, echoed back, in the remorseless intensity with which their relationship is actually lived; yet their union can be achieved only in the act of abandoning the actual world.

Catherine and Heathcliff's love, then, is pushed to the periphery by society itself, projected into myth; yet the fact that it seems *inherently* convertible to myth spotlights the threshold of the novel's 'possible consciousness'. I take that phrase from Lukács and Goldmann to suggest those restrictions set on the consciousness of a historical period which only a transformation of real social relations could abolish – the point at which the most enterprising imagination presses against boundaries which signify not mere failures of personal perception but the limits of what can be historically said. The force Heathcliff symbolises can be truly realised only in some more than merely individualist form; *Wuthering Heights* has its roots not in that narrowed, simplified Romanticism which pits the lonely rebel against an anonymous order, but in that earlier, more authentic Romantic impulse which posits its own kind of 'transindividual' order of value, its own totality, against the order which forces it into exile. Heathcliff may be Byronic, but not in the way Rochester is: the novel counterposes social convention not merely with contrasting personal life-styles but with an alternative world of meaning. Yet it is here that the limits of 'possible consciousness' assert themselves: the offered totalities of Nature, myth and cosmic energy

are forced to figure as asocial worlds unable to engage in more
than idealist ways with the society they subject to judgement.
The price of universality is to be fixed eternally at a point extrinsic to social life – fixed, indeed, at the moment of death,
which both manifests a depth challengingly alien to the Lintons
and withdraws the character from that conventional landscape
into an isolated realm of his own.

Nature, in any case, is no true 'outside' to society, since its
conflicts are transposed into the social arena. In one sense the
novel sharply contrasts Nature and society; in another sense it
grasps civilised life as a higher distillation of ferocious natural
appetite. Nature, then, is a thoroughly ambiguous category, inside
and outside society simultaneously. At one level it represents the
unsalvaged region beyond the pale of culture; at another level it
signifies the all-pervasive reality of which culture itself is a
particular outcropping. It is, indeed, this ambiguity which supplies
the vital link between the childhood and adult phases of Heathcliff's career. Heathcliff the child is 'natural' both because he is
allowed to run wild and because he is reduced as Hindley's
labourer to a mere physical instrument; Heathcliff the adult is
'natural' man in a Hobbesian sense: an appetitive exploiter to
whom no tie or tradition is sacred, a callous predator violently
sundering the bonds of custom and piety. If the first kind of
'naturalness' is anti-social in its estrangement from the norms of
'civilised' life, the second involves the unsociality of one set at
the centre of a world whose social relations are inhuman.
Heathcliff moves from being natural in the sense of an anarchic
outsider to adopting the behaviour natural to an insider in a
viciously competitive society. Of course, to be natural in both
senses is at a different level to be unnatural. From the viewpoint
of culture, it is unnatural that a child should be degraded to a
savage, and unnatural too that a man should behave in the
obscene way Heathcliff does. But culture in this novel is as problematical at Nature. There are no cool Arnoldian touchstones by
which to take the measure of natural degeneracy, since the dialectical vision of *Wuthering Heights* puts culture into question
in the very act of exploring the 'naturalness' which is its negation.
Just as being natural involves being either completely outside
or inside society, as roaming waif or manipulative landlord, so

culture signifies either free-wheeling Romantic fantasy or that well-appointed Linton drawing-room. The adult Heathcliff is the focus of these contradictions: as he worms his way into the social structure he becomes progressively detached in spirit from all it holds dear. But *contradiction* is the essential emphasis. Heathcliff's schizophrenia is symptomatic of a world in which there can be no true dialectic between culture and Nature – a world in which culture is merely refuge from or reflex of material conditions, and so either too estranged from or entwined with those conditions to offer a viable alternative.

I take it that Heathcliff, up to the point at which Cathy rejects him, is in general an admirable character. His account of the Grange adventure, candid, satirical and self-aware as it is, might itself be enough to enforce this point; and we have in any case on the other side only the self-confessedly biased testimony of Nelly Dean. Even according to Nelly's grudging commentary, Heathcliff as a child is impressively patient and uncomplaining (although Nelly adds 'sullen' out of spite), and the heart-rending cry he raises when old Earnshaw dies is difficult to square with her implication that he felt no gratitude to his benefactor. He bears Hindley's vindictive treatment well, and tries pathetically to keep culturally abreast of Catherine despite it. The novel says quite explicitly that Hindley's systematic degradation of Heathcliff 'was enough to make a fiend of a saint';[9] and we should not therefore be surprised that what it does, more precisely, is to produce a pitiless capitalist landlord out of an oppressed child. Heathcliff the adult is in one sense an inversion, in another sense an organic outgrowth, of Heathcliff the child. Heathcliff the child was an isolated figure whose freedom from given genealogical ties offered, as I have argued, fresh possibilities of relationship; Heathcliff the adult is the atomic capitalist to whom relational bonds are nothing, whose individualism is now enslaving rather than liberating. The child knew the purely negative freedom of running wild; the adult, as a man vehemently pursuing ends progressively alien to him, knows only the delusory freedom of exploiting others. The point is that such freedom seems the only kind available in this society, once the relationship with Catherine has collapsed; the only mode of self-affirmation left to Heathcliff is that of oppression which, since it involves self-oppression, is no affirmation at all. Heathcliff is a self-tormentor, a man who is in hell because he can avenge himself on the system which has robbed him of his soul only by battling with it on its own hated terms. If as a child he was outside and inside that system simultaneously, wandering on the moors and working on the farm, he lives out a similar self-division as an adult, trapped in the grinding contradiction between a false social self and the true identity which lies with Catherine. The social self is false, not because Heathcliff is only apparently brutal – that he certainly is – but because it is contradictorily related to the authentic selfhood which is his passion for Catherine. He installs himself at the centre of conventional society, but with wholly negative and inimical intent; his social role is a calculated self-contradiction, created first to further, and then fiercely displace, his asocial passion for Catherine.

Heathcliff's social relation to both Heights and Grange is one of the most complex issues in the novel. Lockwood remarks that he looks too genteel for the Heights; and indeed, in so far as he represents the victory of capitalist property-dealing over the traditional yeoman economy of the Earnshaws, he is inevitably aligned with the world of the Grange. Heathcliff is a dynamic force which seeks to destroy the old yeoman settlement by dispossessing Hareton; yet he does this partly to revenge himself on the very Linton world whose weapons (property deals, arranged marriages) he deploys so efficiently. He does this, moreover, with a crude intensity which is a quality of the Heights world; his roughness and resilience link him culturally to *Wuthering Heights*, and he exploits those qualities to destroy both it and the Grange. He is, then, a force which springs out of the Heights yet subverts it, breaking beyond its constrictions into a new, voracious acquisitiveness. His capitalist brutality is an extension as well as a negation of the Heights world he knew as a child; and to that extent there is continuity between his childhood and adult protests against Grange values, if not against Grange weapons. Heathcliff is subjectively a Heights figure opposing the Grange, and objectively a Grange figure undermining the Heights; he focuses acutely the contradictions between the two worlds. His rise to power symbolises at once the triumph of the oppressed over capitalism and the triumph of capitalism over the oppressed.

He is, indeed, contradiction incarnate – both progressive and outdated, at once caricature of and traditionalist protest against the agrarian capitalist forces of Thrushcross Grange. He harnesses those forces to worst the Grange, to beat it at its own game; but in doing so he parodies that property-system, operates against the Lintons with an unLinton-like explicitness and extremism. He behaves in this way because his 'soul' belongs not to that world but to Catherine; and in that sense his true commitment is an 'outdated' one, to a past, increasingly mythical realm of absolute personal value which capitalist social relations cancel. He embodies a passionate human protest against the marriage-market values of both Grange and Heights at the same time as he callously images those values in caricatured form. Heathcliff exacts vengeance from that society precisely by extravagantly enacting its twisted priorities, becoming a darkly satirical commentary on conventional mores. If he is in one sense a progressive historical force, he belongs in another sense to the superseded world of the Heights, so that his death and the closing-up of the house seem logically related. In the end Heathcliff is defeated and the Heights restored to its rightful owner; yet at the same time the trends he epitomises triumph in the form of the Grange, to which Hareton and young Catherine move away. Hareton wins and loses the Heights simultaneously; dispossessed by Heathcliff, he repossesses the place only to be in that act assimilated by Thrushcross Grange. And if Hareton both wins and loses, then Heathcliff himself is both ousted and victorious.

Quite who has in fact won in the end is a matter of critical contention. Mrs Leavis and Tom Winnifrith both see the old world as having yielded to the new, in contrast to T. K. Meier, who reads the conclusion as 'the victory of tradition over innovation'.[10] The critical contention reflects a real ambiguity in the novel. In one sense, the old values have triumphed over the disruptive usurper: Hareton has wrested back his birthright, and the qualities he symbolises, while preserving their authentic vigour, will be fertilised by the civilising grace which the Grange, in the form of young Catherine, can bring. Heathcliff's career appears from his perspective as a shattering but short-lived interlude, after which true balance may be slowly recovered. In a more obvious sense, however, the Grange has won: the Heights is shut up and Hareton will become the new squire. Heathcliff, then, has been the blunt instrument by which the remnants of the Earnshaw world have been transformed into a fully-fledged capitalist class – the historical medium whereby that world is at once annihilated and elevated to the Grange. Thrushcross values have entered into productive dialogue with rough material reality and, by virtue of this spiritual transfusion, ensured their continuing survival; the Grange comes to the Heights and gathers back to itself what the Heights can yield it. This is why it will not do to read the novel's conclusion as some neatly reciprocal symbolic alliance between the two universes, a symmetrical symbiosis of bourgeois realism and upper-class cultivation. Whatever unity the book finally establishes, it is certainly not symmetrical: in a victory for the progressive forces of agrarian capitalism, Hareton, last survivor of the traditional order, is smoothly incorporated into the Grange.

There is another significant reason why the 'defeat' of Heathcliff cannot be read as the resilient recovery of a traditional world from the injuries it has suffered at his hands. As an extreme parody of capitalist activity, Heathcliff is also an untypical deviation from its norms; as a remorseless, crudely transparent revelation of the real historical character of the Grange, he stands askew to that reality in the very act of becoming its paradigm. It *is* true that Heathcliff, far from signifying some merely ephemeral intervention, is a type of the historically ascendant world of capital; but because he typifies it so 'unnaturally' the novel can move beyond him, into the gracefully gradualistic settlement symbolised by the union of Hareton and young Catherine. Heathcliff is finally fought off, while the social values he incarnates can be prised loose from the self-parodic mould in which he cast them and slowly accommodated. His undisguised violence, like the absolutism of his love, come to seem features of a past more brutal but also more heroic than the present; if the decorous, muted milieu of the Grange will not easily accommodate such passionate intensities, neither will it so readily reveal the more unpleasant face of its social and economic power. The 'defeat' of Heathcliff, then, is at once the transcending of such naked power and the collapse of that passionate protest against it which was the inner secret of Heathcliff's outrageous dealings.

We can now ask what these contradictions in the figure of Heathcliff actually amount to. It seems to me possible to decipher in the struggle between Heathcliff and the Grange an imaginatively transposed version of that contemporary conflict between bourgeoisie and landed gentry which I have argued is central to Charlotte's work. The relationship holds in no precise detail, since Heathcliff is not literally an industrial entrepreneur; but the double-edgedness of his relation with the Lintons, with its blend of antagonism and emulation, reproduces the complex structure of class-forces we found in Charlotte's fiction. Having mysteriously amassed capital outside agrarian society, Heathcliff forces his way into that society to expropriate the expropriators; and in this sense his machinations reflect the behaviour of a contemporary bourgeois class increasingly successful in its penetration of landed property. He belongs fully to neither Heights nor Grange, opposing them both; he embodies a force which at once destroys the traditional Earnshaw settlement and effectively confronts the power of the squirearchy. In his contradictory amalgam of 'Heights' and 'Grange', then, Heathcliff's career fleshes out a contemporary ideological dilemma which Charlotte also explores: the contradiction that the fortunes of the industrial bourgeoisie belong *economically* to an increasing extent with the landed gentry but that there can still exist between them, socially, culturally and personally, a profound hostility. If they are increasingly bound up objectively in a single power-bloc, there is still sharp subjective conflict between them. I take it that *Wuthering Heights*, like Charlotte's fiction, needs mythically to resolve this historical contradiction. If the exploitative adult Heathcliff belongs economically with the capitalist power of the Grange, he is culturally closer to the traditional world of the Heights; his contemptuous response to the Grange as a child, and later to Edgar, is of a piece with Joseph's scorn for the finicky Linton Heathcliff and the haughty young Catherine. If Heathcliff exploits Hareton culturally and economically, he nevertheless feels a certain rough-and-ready *rapport* with him. The contradiction Heathcliff embodies, then, is brought home in the fact that he combines Heights violence with Grange methods to gain power over both properties; and this means that while he is economically progressive he is culturally outdated. He represents a turbulent form of capitalist aggression which must historically be civilised – blended with spiritual values, as it will be in the case of his surrogate Hareton. The

terms into which the novel casts this imperative are those of the
need to refine, in the person of Hareton, the old yeoman class;
but since Hareton's achievement of the Grange is an ironic
consequence of Heathcliff's own activity, there is a sense in which
it is the capitalist drive symbolised by Heathcliff which must submit to spiritual cultivation. It is worth recalling at this point
the cultural affinities between the old yeoman and the new industrial classes touched on by David Wilson;[11] and F. M. L. Thompson comments that by the early 1830s a depleted yeomanry were
often forced to sell their land either to a large landowner, or to a
local tradesman who would put a tenant in.[12] On the other hand,
as Mrs Gaskell notes, some landed yeomen turned to manufacture.
Heathcliff the heartless capitalist and Hareton the lumpish yeoman thus have a real as well as an alliterative relation. In so far as
Heathcliff symbolises the dispossessing bourgeoisie, he links hands
with the large capitalist landowner Linton in common historical
opposition to yeoman society; in so far as he himself has sprung
from that society and turned to amassing capital outside it, still
sharing its dour life-style, he joins spiritual forces with the uncouth Hareton against the pampered squirearchy.

  In pitting himself against both yeomanry and large-scale
agrarian capitalism, then, Heathcliff is an indirect symbol of the
aggressive industrial bourgeoisie of Emily Brontë's own time, a
social trend extrinsic to both classes but implicated in their fortunes. The contradiction of the *novel*, however, is that Heathcliff
cannot represent at once an absolute metaphysical refusal of an
inhuman society and a class which is intrinsically part of it.
Heathcliff is both metaphysical hero, spiritually marooned from
all material concern in his obsessional love for Catherine, and a
skilful exploiter who cannily expropriates the wealth of others. It is
a limit of the novel's 'possible consciousness' that its absolute metaphysical protest can be socially articulated only in such terms – that
its 'outside' is in this sense an 'inside'. The industrial bourgeoisie
is outside the farming world of both Earnshaws and Lintons; but
it is no longer a *revolutionary* class, and so provides no sufficient
social correlative for what Heathcliff 'metaphysically' represents.
He can thus be presented only as a conflictive unity of spiritual
rejection and social integration; and this, indeed, is his personal
tragedy. With this in mind, we can understand why what he did in

that two years' absence has to remain mysterious. The actual facts of his return, as an ambitious *parvenu* armed with presumably non-agrarian wealth and bent on penetrating agrarian society, speak eloquently enough of the real situation of the contemporary bourgeoisie; but it is clear that such social realities offer no adequate symbolism for Heathcliff's unswerving drive, which transcends all social determinants and has its end in Catherine alone. The novel, then, can dramatise its 'metaphysical' challenge to society only by refracting it through the distorting terms of existing social relations, while simultaneously, at a 'deeper' level, isolating that challenge in a realm eternally divorced from the actual.

It seems clear that the novel's sympathies lie on balance with the Heights rather than the Grange. As Tom Winnifrith points out, the Heights is the more homely, egalitarian place; Lockwood's inability at the beginning of the book to work out its social relationships (is Hareton a servant or not?) marks a significant contrast with the Grange. (Lockwood is here a kind of surrogate reader: we too are forestalled from 'reading off' the relationships at first glance, since they are historically moulded and so only historically intelligible.) The passing of the Heights, then, is regretted: it lingers on in the ghostly myth of Heathcliff and Catherine as an unbanishable intimation of a world of hungering absolution askew to the civilised present. Winnifrith declares himself puzzled by Mrs Leavis's point that the action of Hareton and Catherine in replacing the Heights' currant-bushes with flowers symbolises the victory of capitalist over yeoman, but Mrs Leavis is surely right: flowers are a form of 'surplus value', redundant luxuries in the spare Heights world which can accommodate the superfluous neither in its horticulture nor in its social network. But though the novel mourns the death of Wuthering Heights, it invests deeply in the new life which struggles out of it. In so far as Heathcliff signifies a demonic capitalist drive, his defeat is obviously approved; in so far as his passing marks the demise of a life-form rougher but also richer than the Grange, his death symbolises the fleeing of absolute value over the horizon of history into the sealed realm of myth. That death, however tragic, is essential: the future lies with a fusion rather than a confrontation of interests between gentry and bourgeoisie.

The novel's final settlement might seem to qualify what I have said earlier about its confronting of irreconcilable contradictions. *Wuthering Heights* does, after all, end on a note of tentative convergence between labour and culture, sinew and gentility. The culture which Catherine imparts to Hareton in teaching him to read promises equality rather than oppression, an unemasculating refinement of physical energy. But this is a consequence rather than a resolution of the novel's tragic action; it does nothing to dissolve the deadlock of Heathcliff's relationship with Catherine, as the language used to describe that cultural transfusion unconsciously suggests:

> 'Con-*trary*!' said a voice as sweet as a silver bell – 'That for the third time, you dunce! I'm not going to tell you again. Recollect or I'll pull your hair!'
> 'Contrary, then', answered another, in deep but softened tones. 'And now, kiss me, for minding so well.'
> 'No, read it over first correctly, without a single mistake.' The male speaker began to read; he was a young man, respectably dressed and seated at a table, having a book before him. His handsome features glowed with pleasure, and his eyes kept impatiently wandering from the page to a small white hand over his shoulder, which recalled him by a smart slap on the cheek, whenever its owner detected such signs of inattention. Its owner stood behind; her light, shining ringlets blending, at intervals, with his brown locks, as she bent to superintend his studies; and her face – it was lucky he could not see her face, or he would never have been so steady. I could; and I bit my lip in spite, at having thrown away the chance I might have had of doing something besides staring at its smiting beauty.[13]

The aesthetic false moves of this are transparently dictated by ideological compromise. 'Sweet as a silver bell', 'glowed with pleasure', 'shining ringlets', 'smiting beauty': there is a coy, beaming, sentimental self-indulgence about the whole passage which belongs more to Lockwood than to Emily Brontë, although her voice has clearly been confiscated by his. It is Jane and Rochester in a different key; yet the difference is as marked as the parallel. The conclusion, while in a sense symbolically resolving the tragic disjunctions which precede it, moves at a level sufficiently distanced from those disjunctions to preserve their significance

intact. It is true that *Wuthering Heights* finally reveals the limits
of its 'possible consciousness' by having recourse to a gradualist
model of social change: the antinomies of passion and civility will
be harmonised by the genetic fusion of both strains in the offspring of Catherine and Hareton, effecting an equable interchange
of Nature and culture, biology and education. But those possibilities of growth are exploratory and undeveloped, darkened by
the shadow of the tragic action. If it is not exactly true to say that
Hareton and Catherine play Fortinbras to Heathcliff's Hamlet,
since what they symbolise emerges from, rather than merely
imposes itself upon, the narrative, there is none the less a kernel
of truth in that proposition. Hareton and Catherine are the pro-
ducts of their history, but they cannot negate it; the quarrel
between their sedate future at Thrushcross Grange and the spectre
of Heathcliff and Catherine on the hills lives on, in a way alien to
Charlotte's reconciliatory imagination.

  There is another reason why the ending of *Wuthering Heights*
differs from the ideological integration which concludes Charlotte's
novels. I have argued that those novels aim for a balance or fusion
of 'genteel' and bourgeois traits, enacting a growing convergence of
interests between two powerful segments of a ruling social bloc. The
union of Hareton and Catherine parallels this complex unity in
obvious ways: the brash vigour of the petty-bourgeois yeoman is
smoothed and sensitised by the cultivating grace of the squirearchy. But the crucial difference lies in the fact that the yeomanry
of *Wuthering Heights* is no longer a significant class but a historically superannuated force. The transfusion of class-qualities
in Charlotte's case rests on a real historical symbiosis; in *Wuthering Heights* that symbolic interchange has no such solid historical
foundation. The world of the Heights is over, lingering on only in
the figure of Hareton Earnshaw; and in that sense Hareton's
marriage to Catherine signifies more at the level of symbolism
than historical fact, as a salutary grafting of the values of a dying
class on to a thriving, progressive one. If Hareton is thought of as
a surrogate, symbolic Heathcliff, then the novel's ending suggests
a rapprochement between gentry and capitalist akin to Charlotte's
mythical resolutions; if he is taken literally, as a survivor of yeoman stock, then there can be no such historical balance of power.
Literally, indeed, this is what finally happens: Hareton's social

E

class is effectively swallowed up into the hegemony of the Grange. Symbolically, however, Hareton represents a Heathcliff-like robustness with which the Grange must come to terms. It is this tension between literal and symbolic meanings which makes the ending of *Wuthering Heights* considerably more complex than the conclusion of any Charlotte Brontë novel. Read symbolically, the ending of *Wuthering Heights* seems to echo the fusion of qualities found in Charlotte; but since the basis of that fusion is the absorption and effective disappearance of a class on which the novel places considerable value, Emily's conclusion is a good deal more subtly shaded than anything apparent in her sister's work.

*Wuthering Heights* has been alternately read as a social and a metaphysical novel – as a work rooted in a particular time and place, or as a novel preoccupied with the eternal grounds rather than the shifting conditions of human relationship. That critical conflict mirrors a crucial thematic dislocation in the novel itself. The social and metaphysical are indeed ripped rudely apart in the book: existences only feebly incarnate essences, the discourse of ethics makes little creative contact with that of ontology. So much is apparent in Heathcliff's scathing dismissal of Edgar Linton's compassion and moral concern: 'and that insipid, paltry creature attending her from *duty* and *humanity*! From *pity* and *charity*! He might as well plant an oak in a flower-pot, and expect it to thrive, as imagine he can restore her to vigour in the soil of his shallow cares!' The novel's dialectical vision proves Heathcliff both right and wrong. There *is* something insipid about Linton, but his concern for Catherine is not in the least shallow; if his pity and charity are less fertile than Heathcliff's passion, they are also less destructive. But if ethical and ontological idioms fail to mesh, if social existence negates rather than realises spiritual essence, this is itself a profoundly social fact. The novel projects a condition in which the available social languages are too warped and constrictive to be the bearers of love, freedom and equality; and it follows that in such a condition those values can be sustained only in the realms of myth and metaphysics. It is a function of the metaphysical to preserve those possibilities which a society cancels, to act as its reservoir of unrealised value. This is the history of Heathcliff and Catherine – the history of a wedge driven between the actual and the possible which, by estranging the ideal from concrete existence, twists that existence into violence and despair. The actual is denatured to a mere husk of the ideal, the empty shell of some tormentingly inaccessible truth. It is an index of the dialectical vision of *Wuthering Heights* that it shows at once the terror and the necessity of that denaturing, as it shows both the splendour and the impotence of the ideal.

# 7 Anne Brontë

There seems a clear sense in which the categories I have used to analyse Charlotte and Emily's fiction can be extended to Anne Brontë's two novels. *Agnes Grey* and *The Tenant of Wildfell Hall* share a triadic structure: in both cases a pious heroine is flanked by a morally lax upper class on the one hand and a principled hero on the other; and each book ends with her extrication from the clutches of the first and her embracing of the alternative values offered by the second. Agnes Grey is saved from her enslavement as governess to the boorish Bloomfields and insufferable Murrays by marrying the upright young curate Weston; Helen Huntingdon, the tenant of Wildfell Hall, deserts a profligate aristocrat to find happiness with the novel's honest gentleman-farmer hero Gilbert Markham.

The major difference between this structure and the one I have isolated in Charlotte is that it is essentially simple. *Wuthering Heights* also simplifies the structure of Charlotte's fiction to some extent, posing for its heroine a sharp polarity between rebellion (Heathcliff) and conventional authority (Linton); yet Linton is a more subtle character than that label would suggest, and in any case the effect of this 'simplifying' is to raise what remains mixed and ambiguous in Charlotte to the level of a stark, unmitigated battle of tragic forces. The structure of Anne's novels, however, has neither the intriguing ambivalences of Charlotte nor the tragic contradictions of Emily. Charlotte's protagonists are not merely placed, spatially as it were, between two flanking sets of opposing values; they blend both worlds unevenly in their own life-styles, and so struggle self-tormentingly with competing commitments. The irregular dramatic force of the novels springs from this structural complexity – from the 'impure', ambiguous nature of social roles and the personal self-divisions they generate. Anne Brontë's work, by contrast, knows no such internal conflict between the flesh and the spirit. There is one brief moment in *Agnes Grey* when Agnes, dispirited by her fruitless efforts to instil moral principle into the Murrays' spoilt brats, wonders whether her own standards of rectitude might not be insidiously eroded by daily contact with such dissoluteness. But it is a moment only: sustained by her quietly absolute moral convictions, Agnes struggles through to become the wife of a man who lives those convictions with equivalent intensity. Helen Huntingdon's situation is rather more complex, since she has after all been morally blind enough to marry a palpably worthless man; but after that initial error she behaves with impeccable moral sense. Anne Brontë's novels find the world morally mixed, but they do not find morality in the least problematical; *Agnes Grey* and *The Tenant of Wildfell Hall* work on the simple assumption that love, earnestness and evangelical truth are preferable to social achievement and can, with sufficient long-suffering, be attained.

This ethic marks Anne off in different ways from both Charlotte and Emily. Charlotte's novels dramatise a conflict betwen 'morality' and society', but the two sets of values are subtly intertwined, so that to live well involves both eagerly embracing the world and firmly fending it off. Her protagonists are fascinated and repelled by social achievement, torn between asceticism and ambition, covertly seduced by the very Society world they find puritanically distasteful. It is because the novels find that world so alluring that they are so bitter about it – so quick to remonstrate and reprove, with a mixture of honest dissent and rationalised envy. Whereas Lucy Snowe's chiding of Polly Home and Ginevra Fanshawe betrays less reputable motives than mere moral disinterestedness, Agnes Grey admonishes her obnoxious charges with a remarkable freedom from personal malice – the more remarkable because we have in this work a more direct and detailed account of the social violence to which the governess is subjected than anything we find elsewhere in the Brontës. The essence of that violence is the employer's operation of a 'double bind' system, whereby whatever action or response the governess initiates is automatically nullified in the name of some alternative, equally unviable mode of behaviour. The governess is expected

to keep her pupils in order but deprived of the authority to do so
lest she forget her lowly status; she must report their progress to
their mother but refrain from criticising them for fear of alienat-
ing the maternal good favour on which her livelihood depends. If
she imposes discipline she impudently usurps parental privilege;
if she assumes a liberal posture she risks dismissal on the grounds
of professional laxity. Her fraught relation to her pupils, then,
provides a painfully lucid image of 'genteel' poverty's unwilling
alliance with morally irresponsible wealth.

Yet Agnes's account of her agonised career as governess is all
the more poignant for its patient, unruffled objectivity – an objectivity which neither slides over her sufferings in sham-heroic silence
(she is ready enough to confess hurt pride, anger and exaspera-
tion) nor spreads a thin film over bitter, bottled-up resentment.
The reason why Agnes's responses are cooler, more equable than
those we find in a Charlotte protagonists's truck with the gentry
is because her own *amour-propre* is not fundamentally at stake.
Agnes's own social feelings are not significantly invested in the
situation; and she is thus detached from that situation in
a way impossible for Charlotte's heroines. She exists in the
first place as a moral rather than a social being; and moral
principle, while strictly applicable to social manners, is in the end
self-validating and self-sufficient, grounded in God alone. This is
not, as it occasionally is with Charlotte, a question of smugness –
of that self-righteous falling back on simple evangelical virtue
which is in fact a devious form of aggression, a provocative parade
of one's exasperating invulnerability. For such a resolutely moral
writer, Anne Brontë is remarkably unsmug; Agnes Grey can
humbly commend her own moral excellence with the judicious
impersonality she shows in evaluating the qualities of others. '. . . I
was the only person in the house who steadily professed good
principles, habitually spoke the truth, and generally endeavoured
to make inclination bow to duty; and this I say, not, of course, in
commendation of myself, but to show the unfortunate state of the
family to which my services were, for the present, devoted.'[1] The
plain-minded integrity of Edward Weston reveals a moral value
which Charlotte's protagonists would of course find admirable; but
they would also, one feels, find him ponderous in a way that *Agnes*

*Grey* does not. *Jane Eyre* would no doubt feel towards Agnes as it does towards Helen Burns; it is excellent to adhere to ascetic principles when you are not long for this world anyway.

There is, on the other hand, a significant difference between Anne and Emily. If Anne's novels focus on an opposition between world and spirit, between authentic love and upper-class marriage market, so in a sense does *Wuthering Heights*. But the determinant structure of *Wuthering Heights* is for one thing less morally simple; there is more to say about the Lintons and the Earnshaws than that they play the marriage market, and Edgar Linton is hardly an Arthur Huntingdon. But if the moral issues of *Wuthering Heights* are less clear-cut, this is partly because the novel contains a structural opposition, not only (as with Anne) between vice and virtue, but between the ethical itself and forms of passional energy which put it into radical question. It is for this reason that, while the conflict between 'world' and 'spirit' in *Wuthering Heights* is at one level more complex than in Anne Brontë, it is also in another sense sharper, tougher, more recalcitrant to resolution. Emily's novel, *pace* the neo-Nietzscheans, subtly enforces moral discriminations, but does so within a perspective which entertains more radical counterpositions – between, say, passion and morality itself. To put the matter over-succinctly: if *Wuthering Heights* contains a contradiction between love and social morality, Anne Brontë's novels turn on a contrast between society and moral love. The sharpness of both oppositions marks the two sisters off from Charlotte; but whereas in Emily's work there can be no realised social solution to the major tragic conflict, Anne leans towards a Charlotte-like position in her quiet concluding optimism. In *Agnes Grey* and *The Tenant*, love is finally vindicated; it must disengage itself from Society, but not from the common social world. The love of Heathcliff and Catherine has at its disposal no world of social value outside Grange and Heights in which it might be socially nurtured and articulated; in Charlotte's fiction there are conflicting strata of social values, so that, say, an animus against the aristocracy may find expression in petty-bourgeois puritanism, but the thrust of the novels is towards some rapprochement between these levels. Anne's novels occupy a third position which combines something of both: there *are* other clusters of social value to which one may have recourse

in flight from the depredations of the gentry; but there is no particular drive towards establishing any creative liaison between
these antagonistic social worlds.

The action of *Agnes Grey* is fundamentally simple; in the spare
lucidity of its narrative it is, indeed, something of a classic
distillation of a Brontë structure of feeling. Its final line – 'And
now I think I have said sufficient' – neatly captures the laconic
modesty of the whole, the sense of a work attractively reserved
in feeling without any loss of candid revelation. Agnes is the
daughter of a fairly affluent propertied clergyman who married a
squire's daughter, and so has a vaguely aristocratic lineage; but
whereas Charlotte's similar upgradings of her protagonists' social
status* involve a degree of wish-fulfilment, Mrs Grey's genteel
background seems introduced only to show how irrelevant it is in
comparison with 'human' considerations. Agnes's father fails to
appreciate this fully:

> My father, however, whose temper was neither tranquil nor
> cheerful by nature, often unduly vexed himself with thinking of
> the sacrifices his dear wife had made for him; and troubled his
> head with revolving endless schemes for the augmentation of his
> little fortune, for her sake and ours. In vain my mother assured
> him she was quite satisfied; and if he would but lay by a little
> for the children, we should all have plenty, both for time
> present and to come: but saving was not my father's forte.[2]

The result of Mr Grey's needless anxiety over his wife is specula-
tion and financial ruin – a clear enough indication that social
rank is a poor second to love. It is the loss of his fortunes which
forces Agnes into the world of the *arriviste* Bloomfields and arrogant Murrays;† and the novel then revolves around a simple
contrast between vain, shallow, egoistic upper-class life and the
virtues of compassion and integrity displayed by both Agnes and
Edward Weston. Those virtues are of course 'classless' – Mrs

---

* Upgrading, I mean, in relation to the Brontës' own social class.

† It is interesting that Agnes becomes a governess not, as in Charlotte
Brontë, to *escape* from a claustrophobic domestic set-up, or because ties
of kinship have mysteriously melted away, but to *help* her family. She
responds enthusiastically to the stimulating prospect of a new life, but there
is no suggestion of chafing ambition.

Grey remarks unexceptionally that there is good and bad to be found in all social classes – but it is implicit in the novel's structure that they are most readily found in the pious, working petty bourgeoisie of whom Agnes and Weston are both representative. They certainly aren't easily locatable in the vulgar *nouveau riche* Bloomfields or the aristocratic Murrays; and a major index of virtue is in fact the straight class-issue of how one treats the poor. The Murray daughters, predictably, treat their father's cottagers like animals:

> They would watch the poor creatures at their meals, making uncivil remarks about their food, and their manner of eating; they would laugh at their simple notions and provincial expressions, till some of them scarcely durst venture to speak; they would call the grave elderly men and women old fools and silly old blockheads to their faces; and all this without meaning to offend.[8]

That final unpredictable phrase is significant: it charitably tempers the cutting-edge of Agnes's class-judgement on the gentry, but does so ironically by a fatalistic appeal to the fact of class as an excuse for the girls' behaviour. Cultivated young ladies like the Murrays simply cannot be expected to put themselves in the place of the poor: 'They thought that, as these cottagers were poor and untaught, they must be stupid and brutish. . . .'[4] Agnes tries to extirpate these false concepts, but without avail; morality must do what it can, but in the end it is impotent against the crass moral stupidity of the ruling class. While one is on the inside of the gentry's world one must morally reprove it as a matter of duty; but it cannot really be changed, and the only answer is disengagement: Agnes goes off to marry Weston. There is no way in which petty-bourgeois puritanism can penetrate the ears of the morally lax loungers who own most of England. The aristocratic world has to be left as it is; it is notable that Rosalie Murray, having achieved her aim of marrying Sir Thomas Ashby and been made thoroughly miserable in the process, is almost as morally unregenerate as ever when Agnes visits her at Ashby Park. (It is also notable that Agnes's visit makes a general moral point, rather than, like Jane's return to the Reeds, indulging an unconscious private malice in seeing them so broken.) In marrying a clergyman, Agnes re-enacts her parents' settlement, returns to spiritual base rather than progressing up the social scale.

*Agnes Grey*, then, is ambivalent about how far morality is *class*-morality. Officially, of course, it isn't: Anne Brontë is hardly taking the line that only the petty bourgeoisie will enter the kingdom of God. In principle, any class may see the light; there are even twinges of regeneracy in the loathsome Rosalie. Implicitly, however, it is clear that there is a close bond between class and morality: the lower your rung on the social (and, to some extent, ecclesiastical) ladder, the more virtuous you are likely to be. It is best, then, to keep clear of fashionable moral laxity, never attempting (as the final paragraph admonishes) to imitate one's richer neighbours. *Agnes Grey* argues on the one hand the position of Agnes's parents – that class does not matter to love, that moral piety cuts across factitious social interests. Agnes, accordingly, withdraws from her enforced entanglement with social privilege to marry a pure embodiment of morality, a cleric. But on the other hand class clearly *does* matter, since the social arrogance of the aristocracy is so translucently expressed in their moral shabbiness. Love and morality can thus be realised only in a commitment to the values of piety, plainness, duty and sobriety, which the novel shows to have obvious petty-bourgeois roots. It is simply that the book refuses to admit these class-determinants, clinging instead to a direct counterposing of moral principle to any kind of social interest. There is no assertive Jane Eyre-like 'keep to your caste', no self-consolatory social retreat; you *do* in fact retreat to your own class, away from a morally dubious aristocracy, but this is presented as an absolute stand on moral imperatives which transcend class altogether.

Such a prudent retreat might seem false of *The Tenant of Wildfell Hall*; for at the end of that novel, as Gilbert Markham is elevated to the squirearchy, we have something which looks very much like a convergence of social classes. Markham is the son of a gentleman farmer, and ambitious to boot: his father has tried to counter the restless impulses bred in Gilbert by a socially ambitious mother, and the novel opens with Markham's tight-lipped struggle to divert his desire for self-improvement into pragmatic plans for the improvement of agriculture. At the end of the book, having conquered certain qualms of social presumption and married Helen Huntingdon, he has become squire of the sizeable park and mansion of Staningley. It looks, then, like a version of the conclusion of *Wuthering Heights* – the stolid values of the yeomanry strategically infused into the squirearchy. And yet in reading the novel this is hardly the way it appears at all. For one thing, Helen's obscure social origins render her status as traditional gentry problematical; and Gilbert is in any case hardly a Hareton Earnshaw. The over-socialised environment of his home has little in common with the gaunt gracelessness of Wuthering Heights. He may be a gentleman farmer, but he is more gentleman than farmer; we do, admittedly, see him once with his sleeves rolled up in a corn-field and hear him planning extensive field-drainage, but he is more typically to be found handing around the cream and sugar in the drawing-room. The early Gilbert would be more at home in Cranford than Wuthering Heights, a fact enforced by the deliberate falseness of tone with which he and his domestic context are presented. There is a gossipy, self-indulgent, complacent domesticity about the Markham family which is intended to put the reader on guard:

> However, that haven of bliss must not be entered till I had exchanged my miry boots for a clean pair of shoes, and my rough surtout for a respectable coat, and made myself generally presentable before decent society; for my mother, with all her kindness, was vastly particular on certain points.
>
> In ascending to my room, I was met upon the stairs by a smart, pretty girl of nineteen, with a tidy, dumpy figure, a round face, bright blooming cheeks, glossy clustering curls, and little merry brown eyes, I need not tell you this was my sister Rose. She is, I know, a comely matron still, and, doubtless, no less lovely – in your eyes – than on the happy day you first beheld her.[5]

If the first paragraph places domestic decency in unsubtly ironic brackets, the secret of that irony's laboured archness is betrayed in the subsequent portrait of Rose, which is straightforwardly coy. There follows a cosy scene in which the family take tea, supervised by a mother ('that honoured lady') who is described with the same mixture of ironic jocoseness and covert sentimentalism. The whole tableau is calculatedly fussy; and the effect is underscored by Gilbert's brother Fergus, whose boorishness is meant to offer a sardonic contrast with his delicately-minded kin. He is discussing the new tenant of the Hall with his mother:

'. . . mind you bring me word how much sugar she puts in her tea, and what sort of caps and aprons she wears, and all about it; for I don't know how I can live till I know', said Fergus, very gravely.

But if he intended the speech to be hailed as a master-stroke of wit, he signally failed, for nobody laughed. However, he was not much disconcerted at that; for when he had taken a mouthful of bread and butter, and was about to swallow a gulp of tea, the humour of the thing burst upon him with such irresistible force, that he was obliged to jump up from the table, and rush snorting and choking from the room; and a minute after, was heard screaming in fearful agony in the garden.[6]

Fergus may be as crude as his chunk of bread, but his gruffness is merely a licensed jesting which slots neatly into the family circle, supplying the others with a source of comfortably whimsical humour.

Gilbert himself is foolishly sentimental; and since it is he and not the novel who maintains that, though 'a little bit spoiled by [his] mother and sister, and some other ladies of [his] acquaintance', he is 'by no means a fop',[7] we can take it that the book, in allowing him to protest too much, has serious reservations about his character. He is touchy and overbred, full of rhetorical gestures and gallant clichés, alternating between tender idealisations and bursts of histrionic wrath. He is, in fact, emotionally infantile, ready to 'stamp with vexation' when his candle won't light, falling easily into self-pitying misanthropy as a rejected lover, quick to inflict grotesque violence on Helen's brother Mr Lawrence. The novel's contrast, then, is between the over-civilised world of the gentleman farmer's family around the tea-table, and the bitter human tragedy with which Gilbert is brought into contact by the arrival of Helen Huntingdon at Wildfell Hall. In this sense the book inverts the situation of *Wuthering Heights*: here it is the yeomen who are febrile, and the socially superior Helen (sister of the local squire) who represents a bleak world of mental torture. The contrast is enforced in the argument over whether Helen is right to deny her son Arthur alcoholic drink:

'I have been accustomed to make him swallow a little wine or weak spirits-and-water, by way of medicine when he was sick, and, in fact, I have done what I could to make him hate them.' Everybody laughed, except the young widow and her son. 'Well, Mrs Graham', said my mother, wiping the tears of merriment from her bright blue eyes — 'well, you surprise me! I really gave you credit for having more sense — The poor child will be the veriest milksop that ever was sopped!'[8]

Once the truth of Helen's history is out, that laugh will go against the Markham circle as a sign of moral frivolousness; what seems to them pointlessly puritanical will become intelligible when the facts are known. This helps to portray the Markhams as shallow beside Helen's unfashionable gravity, and as unselfcritical too: what title has Mrs Markham to complain about rearing a child as a milksop?

The effect of this inversion of the *Wuthering Heights* set-up is that the bonds between 'social' and 'moral' are loosened. Whereas in *Wuthering Heights* moral qualities are subtly entwined with distinct kinds of social and economic relations, in the contrast between the working environment of the Heights and the squire-archical Grange, *The Tenant* portrays a working world which is overbred and a non-working context (Wildfell Hall) which is steeped in grimness and gloom. What the book does, in other words, is to take the geographical setting of Emily's novel — the Grange in the lush valley, the Heights on the hill — and invert its *social* content, so that the yeomanry live among wooded valleys and meadow-lands while the genteel Helen inhabits 'the wildest and the loftiest eminence' in the region:

I left the more frequented regions, the wooded valleys, the corn-fields and the meadow-lands, and proceeded to mount the steep acclivity of Wildfell . . . where, as you ascend, the hedges, as well as the trees, become scanty and stunted, the former, at length, giving place to rough stone fences, partly greened over with ivy and moss, the latter to larches and Scotch fir-trees, or isolated blackthorns. The fields, being rough and stony, and

wholly unfit for the plough, were mostly devoted to the pastur-
ing of sheep and cattle; the soil was thin and poor: bits of
grey rock here and there peeped out from the grassy hill-
ocks. . . .[9]

'Social' and 'moral' are interconnected in that the Markhams'
comfortably mannered life-style has its roots in the wealth yielded
by fertile land – just as the Earnshaws' thin-bloodedness is bound
up with the thinness of their soil. But if Wildfell Hall is Wuthering Heights, then it is clear that what Emily's work presents as a
seamlessly moral and social universe is reduced by Anne to a
merely moral issue. The dreariness of Wildfell Hall is symbolic
merely of one individual's suffering, not, as with Wuthering
Heights, the hardy endurance of a whole class; it projects a state
of moral consciousness rather than a social reality. Helen Huntingdon is not a 'representative' character as Hindley Earnshaw is;
and neither is Gilbert Markham. We cannot say of him, as we can
of Hareton, that his personal biography richly embodies the complex movement of deeper social trends.

This partial unhinging of the 'moral' from a nurturing social
context is evident too in the doomed relationship between Helen
and Arthur Huntingdon. Helen's social roots are fairly obscure;
although her father leaves her little money she is clearly 'gentry'
and moves in Society circles before meeting Arthur; but, as Tom
Winnifrith points out,[10] her brother Mr Lawrence is not too grand
to be on easy social terms with Gilbert, and although Gilbert
thinks twice about aspiring by marriage to Helen's elevated position, the marriage is not in any palpable way disapproved of by
the 'world'. Helen's relationship with Arthur, then, is not notably
unequal; and this means that, in contrast with the Jane–Rochester
liaison, it moves primarily within a moral domain. The analogy
with *Jane Eyre* is necessarily inexact, since Arthur is vicious and
Rochester merely flawed; but both encounters involve a libertine
aristocrat and a morally conscientious woman. In Charlotte's
novel, however, the moral conflict is fuelled and deepened by the
facts of social inequality, in a complex drama of tensions and
alliances. Like Jane, Helen has 'rooted principles in favour of a
plain, dark, sober style of dress';[11] and in this sense her moral
responses have a similar petty-bourgeois class-basis. Her reaction

to the motley crew of raffish idlers who hang around her husband is not far removed from Agnes Grey's distaste for the becurled, toadying High Churchman Hatfield. But the fact that Helen is not literally lower middle-class, is socially much closer to Arthur's world than Jane is to Rochester's, empties the relationship of social substance and defuses it to a timeless moral fable. As in *Agnes Grey*, social and moral are prised apart in the protagonist's consciousness at the same time as they are conflated in the behaviour of her superiors. There is a dramatically direct correlation between class and moral character in the dissipated Arthur and his cronies, but it is too direct, too undialectical: Arthur is little more than a stereotype of the traditional wicked aristocrat.

Helen, then, is socially genteel but spiritually not; she has to be of 'high' birth for plot purposes, in order plausibly to marry Arthur in the first place, but her moral life has much in common with the suffering sobriety and patient self-possession of the socially inferior Agnes Grey. She is, indeed, as much of a morally outraged outsider in the riotous world of Grassdale Manor as Agnes is in the Murrays' Horton Lodge; and in that sense her final union with Gilbert Markham has no representative social significance, not least because the social gap between them is nothing like that between Hareton and young Catherine. In the end, it is merely a matter of love winning out, as it did with the socially unequal parents of Agnes Grey. It is true that marriage meant a social fall for them and means a social rise for Gilbert; but whether you slide up or down, the main point remains that you must love where you truly love, undistracted by social distinctions. In principle, class does not matter; in practice it does, since the upper classes are both unloving and unlovable. Helen, therefore, needs to be morally disengaged by the novel from her own class, and in the end physically extricated from it by turning to Gilbert. That extrication might seem more ambiguous in *The Tenant* than in *Agnes Grey*, since the novel ends with Gilbert and Helen climbing, as it were, back in. But this is unimportant, since the novel is essentially a love-story and a moral fable, not a history of convergent class-interests. Neither Helen nor Gilbert are presented as embodiments of class-forces: Helen, as I have argued, is made deliberately untypical, and Gilbert figures throughout as frustrated lover rather than representative of the yeomanry. Indeed, the fact that the first-person narration gives us immediate access to Markham's distraught consciousness signifies the book's concern with him as psychologically interesting individual rather than as social symbol. He contrasts in this sense with Edward Weston, who is treated with thorough externality as a moral type.

There seem to me two major reasons, both implicit in the analysis I have given, why the orthodox critical judgement that Anne Brontë's work is slighter than her sisters' is just. The first concerns the essential simplicity of the structural relations her novels set up. I have argued that *Agnes Grey* and *The Tenant of Wildfell Hall* pivot on a simple binary opposition between immoral gentry and righteous protagonist – an opposition between life-styles which are objectively bound up with social class. This is easy to see if we examine the aristocratic side of the conflict: it just is the case that such parasitic living breeds a moral slackness which veers easily into outright viciousness. But as I have claimed, the novels less readily admit the other side of the equation – that their moral positives are similarly shot through with social ideology. And this suppresses the intricate interweavings of attraction and repulsion we find in Charlotte, at the same time as it by-passes the passionate conflicts we find in Emily. Anne's fiction manifests a strenuous struggle between society and authentic value, but the struggle is not internalised, as it is with Jane Eyre and Catherine Earnshaw. Agnes Grey merely retires from the field of social combat to find peace with Weston; she lives out no personal crisis of contradictory values. Helen Huntingdon *is* emotionally involved with the aristocracy to the point of having married one of its more disreputable members; but once the adulterous Arthur is revealed for what he is, she knows no inward turmoil of allegiance – as, say, Caroline Helstone hesitates between her love for and moral doubts about Robert Moore. She merely adopts a consistent moral posture which renders her an internal exile within the drunken brawls of Grassdale Manor. Anne Brontë's charity – a virtue Charlotte finds notably difficult – is coupled with a stoical passivity, a lack of that dynamic self-assertion which in Charlotte's work provides the very stuff of dramatic conflict. *Agnes Grey* is something like a *Jane Eyre* with Helen Burns as the heroine. St John Rivers, in his intense evangelical virtue, has something of the attractions of Edward Weston, but he is also a good deal less restful, so that the flight from aristocratic vice which in *Agnes Grey* lands you in the arms of a ready-made moral solution opens up in *Jane Eyre* a whole new area of strife and self-division. *Agnes Grey* seems to me a successful novel, despite the slightness seized on by contemporary reviewers; the point is that its success thrives on its slightness, on a spare, humble lucidity which involves expelling those heated emotional entanglements brought to the surface by Charlotte.

*The Tenant of Wildfell Hall* encloses Helen's first-person version of her marriage to Arthur within Gilbert's own account of this, and his courtship in general, to his friend Halford. The effect of this structural device is unfortunate: it seems to convert the novel's most substantial, emotionally engaging section – the *Agnes Grey* part of it, as it were – into a mere mechanism to further Gilbert's courtship, since the information Helen's account of her life discloses – why she is apparently frigid and elusive, why she is so intimate with Gilbert's supposed rival Lawrence – persuades Markham that he can go ahead and win her. What is literally and imaginatively central to the book is formally de-centred by the novel's curious structure, which throws into formal predominance the courtship: the stereotyped Romantic saga of the cold mistress and the baffled lover. The disjunction is focused in Markham's callously inadequate reaction to Helen's harrowing tale: 'not that I was at all insensible to Mrs Huntingdon's wrongs or unmoved by her sufferings, but, I must confess, I felt a kind of selfish gratification in watching her husband's gradual decline in her good graces, and seeing how completely he extinguished all her affection at last'.[12] His blatantly self-interested response to Helen's history is as unpleasant as the wallowings in egoistic joy into which he is thrown a moment later. Rochester's recounting of his past to Jane makes a significant contrast: the episode successfully serves the twin purposes of illuminating the mysterious aristocrat and furthering his pursuit of Jane. This, formally, is the intention of Helen's autobiography too; but its length and fascination gain the upper hand, pushing into the background the considerably less interesting formal structure of Romantic courtship within which it is set. Helen is so obviously morally and artistically superior to Gilbert, and the Grassdale episode so much more gripping than the context in which it is set, that some odd structural inversion seems to have occurred. What is officially an interlude becomes the guts of the book, displacing the framework which surrounds it.

That structural incongruity has its significance. By enfolding the Grassdale events within a traditional love-story, the novel once more dissolves the social to the individual, diverting a confrontation of class-values to an exploration of personal suffering and self-fulfilment. A contrast with *Wuthering Heights* is useful here. That novel also, of course, exploits the device of narrative-within-narrative, but to very different effect. There is a certain surface parallelism between Gilbert Markham's early visits to Helen at the Hall and Lockwood's first visit to the Heights. In both cases an over-civilised, well-meaning but slightly foolish guest is uncomfortably thrown by the churlish suspicion he encounters in his host. In both novels there then follows an unravelling of past history – an extended account of why the host is in fact so brusque. But Lockwood listens to Nelly's tale merely to enable the tale to be told; it does not concern him personally, beyond satisfying a certain curiosity. The story is told for the reader, not for Lockwood. In *The Tenant*, however, the story is recounted wholly for Gilbert, as Helen's way of explaining and apologising for her cool treatment of him; and this gives Gilbert an importance as a character which he seems to deserve hardly more than Lockwood. Gilbert seems in part a Lockwood moved to the centre of the stage; but though he formally occupies that privileged spot, the true drama of the novel is conducted elsewhere. By choosing such a character for its protagonist, the novel is unable to make much more than a Romantic fable out of its suggestive social materials.

Anne Brontë's relative separation of the personal and social seems to me the second reason for the slightness of her fiction. If the unique richness of individual character lies precisely in its complex manifold of relations, then Anne's novels suffer in a comparison with the work of her sisters. In the personal relationships of *Wuthering Heights* we feel continuously the inward, enriching pressure of social reality, swaddling and shaping individual destinies; there is hardly a character in the novel who is not, in a Lukácsian sense, 'typical', linked by capillary fibres to the central

nerves of history. Charlotte Brontë is less consistent in achieving such typicality: Edward Crimsworth, Job Barraclough, Blanche
Ingram and Madame Walravens are symptomatic rather than
representative figures, and even Shirley's status must be judged
ambiguous in this respect. But Jane, Rochester, Caroline, Hunsden,
Lucy: these are characters who can neither be reduced to nor
dissevered from a nurturing matrix of historical life. It is this
dimension which Anne's fiction seems to lack, so that her novels
appear in the end merely 'moral', despite the social scenarios
within which those moral dilemmas are posed. Her aristocratic
figures, for example, are purely symptomatic: Mr Murray is 'a
blustering, roystering, country squire; a devoted fox-hunter, a
skilful horse-jockey and farrier, an active, practical farmer, and a
hearty *bon-vivant*';[18] and that self-generating inventory of stereotyped upper-class pursuits is about as much as we ever know of
him. If the aristocratic villains are mechanically reducible to their
social determinants, the protagonists are too abstractly individu-
ated, too internally unpressured by the strains and frictions of
their social world. It is for this reason that the union of Helen
and Gilbert can articulate nothing of that questioning sense of
fundamental values, and of the social tissue in which they are
embedded, which communicates itself so powerfully in the coming
together of Hareton and Catherine.

Anne Brontë's novels seem to allot little space to what we think
of as perhaps the most dominant of all Brontë categories – the
imagination. For the imagination in Charlotte and Emily is a
sacred, subversive force – one which goads you outwards and onwards towards an unfathomable fulfilment, and at the same time
plunges you vertiginously into the seething depths of the self. The
language of Anne Brontë's work is that of morality rather than
imagination: her fiction is concerned neither with submerged
depths nor with far horizons, but with the criteria by which men
and women should act well. And yet, if this voids her writing of
the high drama of *Jane Eyre* and *Wuthering Heights*, imbuing
her first book with a greyness candidly acknowledged in the title,
it does not involve some prudish shirking of real issues. If her work
lacks the *brio* of Emily's, it also lacks the compromise of Charlotte's; if it shares Charlotte's anxious autobiographical realism,

it also shares Emily's sense of certain conflicts in which no accommodation is possible. If Anne is in every sense more charitable than Charlotte, she is in other ways almost as toughly clear-sighted as Emily.

# Notes

## Introduction

1. F. R. and Q. D. Leavis, *Lectures in America* (London, 1969) p. 131.

2. London, 1973, p. 1.

3. 'Criticism as a Humanist Discipline', in *Contemporary Criticism*, ed. M. Bradbury and D. Palmer (London, 1970) p. 57.

4. Vol. I (reprinted London, 1971) p. 431.

5. *Labouring Men* (London, 1964) p. 29.

6. Quoted by David Wilson, 'Emily Brontë: First of the Moderns', *Modern Quarterly Miscellany*, no. 1 (1947). I am indebted to Mr Wilson's article for several of these historical details.

7. *The Life of Charlotte Brontë*, ed. Ward and Shorter, p. 48.

8. For Goldmann's use of the concept, see in particular 'The Sociology of Literature: Status and Problems of Method', *International Social Science Journal*, XIX, no. 4 (1967). Goldmann's model of 'mediations' between text and society seems to me considerably too simple and symmetrical, overstressing the transparency with which each 'level' shines through the others. His whole notion of structure has been implic-itly criticised by Pierre Marcherey in his *Pour une Théorie de la Production Littéraire* (Paris, 1966), although I disagree with Macherey's outright rejection of the notion of 'immanent' literary structure.

9. My main sources for the following brief, schematic account are: F. M. L. Thompson, *English Landed Society in the Nineteenth Century* (London, 1963); J. T. Ward and R. G. Wilson (eds.), *Land and Industry: The Landed Estate and the Industrial Revolution* (London, 1971); F. M. L. Thompson, 'Whigs and Liberals in the West Riding, 1830–1860', *English Historical Review* (1959), and 'Land and Politics in the Nineteenth Century', *Transactions of the Royal Historical Society* (1965); J. T. Ward, 'West Riding Landowners and the Corn Laws', *English Historical Review* (1966); H. J. Perkin, *The Origins of Modern English Society, 1780–1880* (London, 1969); C. H. E. Zangerl, 'Social Composition of the County Magistracy of England and Wales, 1831–1887', *Journal of British Studies* (1971).

10. See E. Neff, *Carlyle and Mill* (New York, 1926) p. 67.

11. *Historical Materialism*, in *Marx and Engels: Basic Writings on*

# 140 Notes

*Politics and Philosophy*, ed. L. S. Feuer (London, 1972) p. 97.

12. *The Problem of Method* (London, 1963) p. 56.

13. See *For Marx* (London, 1969) part III: 'Contradiction and Over-determination'.

14. See William Wright, *The Brontës in Ireland* (London, 1896). pp. 252–4.

15. Tom Winnifrith, *The Brontës and their Background: Romance and Reality* (London, 1973) p. 148.

16. See *The Brontës: Their Lives, Friendships and Correspond-ence*, ed. Wise and Symington (London, 1932) vol. I, p. 162.

17. Winnifrith, p. 156.

18. Wise and Symington, vol. I, p. 177.

19. Winnifrith, p. 153.

20. Wise and Symington, vol. I, p. 139.

21. Winifred Gerin, *Branwell Brontë* (London, 1961) p. 24.

22. ibid., p. 128.

23. Wilson, in *Mod. Q. Misc.*, no. 1 (1947).

24. *Life of Charlotte Brontë*, pp. 19–20.

## Chapter 1: Jane Eyre

1. *Jane Eyre*, ed. Ward and Shorter, ch. 6, pp. 62–3.
2. Ch. 4, p. 32.
3. Ch. 24, p. 331.
4. Ch. 7, p. 75.
5. *Villette*, ed. Ward and Shorter, ch. 8, p. 87.
6. Ch. 2, p. 9.
7. Ch. 12, p. 123.
8. *Shirley*, ed. Ward and Shorter, ch. 7, p. 113.
9. *The Professor*, ed. Ward and Shorter, ch. 3, p. 24.
10. *Jane Eyre*, ch. 16, p. 192.
11. Ch. 2, p. 14.
12. Ch. 32, p. 458.
13. Ch. 21, p. 286.
14. Ch. 11, p. 118.
15. Ch. 30, p. 433.
16. Ch. 30, p. 429.
17. Ch. 30, p. 430.
18. Ch. 34, p. 487.
19. Ch. 12, p. 129.
20. Ch. 34, p. 498.
21. Ch. 34, p. 496.
22. Ch. 35, p. 508.
23. Ch. 31, p. 442.
24. Ch. 37, p. 546.
25. Ch. 27, p. 286.
26. Ch. 35, p. 506.
27. Ch. 1, p. 5.
28. Ch. 2, p. 13.
29. Ch. 4, p. 37.
30. Ch. 23, p. 310.
31. Ch. 10, p. 98.
32. Ch. 17, p. 210.
33. Ch. 2, p. 12.
34. Ch. 17, p. 194.
35. Ch. 11, p. 118.
36. Ch. 3, p. 22.
37. Ch. 31, p. 438.
38. Ch. 34, p. 475.
39. Ch. 31, p. 439.
40. Ch. 29, p. 416.
41. Ch. 23, p. 308.
42. Ch. 24, p. 326.
43. Ch. 23, p. 307.
44. Ch. 37, p. 549
45. Ch. 37, p. 534.
46. Ch. 17, p. 215.
47. Ch. 16, pp. 187–8.

### Chapter 2: The Professor

1. *Jane Eyre*, ch. 32, p. 458
2. *The Professor*, ed. Ward and Shorter, ch. 25, p. 254.
3. Ch. 1, pp. 6–7.
4. Ch. 1, p. 7.
5. Ch. 2, p. 15.
6. Ch. 1, p. 7.
7. Ch. 2, pp. 18–19.
8. Ch. 4, p. 31.
9. Ch. 3, p. 26.
10. Ch. 2, p. 16.
11. Ch. 4, p. 35.
12. Ch. 3, p. 28.
13. Ch. 3, p. 28.
14. Ch. 4, p. 37.
15. Ch. 3, p. 28.
16. Ch. 3, pp. 28–9.
17. Ch. 4, p. 38.
18. Ch. 24, pp. 241–2, 245–6.
19. Ch. 10, p. 90.
20. Ch. 10, p. 90.
21. Ch. 3., p. 23.
22. Ch. 12, p. 106.
23. Ch. 13, p. 114.
24. Ch. 15, p. 129.
25. Ch. 15, p. 131.
26. Ch. 16, p. 134.
27. Ch. 8, p. 69.
28. Ch. 24, p. 249.
29. Ch. 25, p. 252.
30. Ch. 15, p. 127.
31. Ch. 19, p. 182.
32. Ch. 18, p. 152.
33. Preface, p. 3
34. See G. Lukács, *The Historical Novel* (London, 1962) chs. 1–2.

### Chapter 3: Shirley

1. See J. F. C. Harrison, 'Chartism in Leeds', in Asa Briggs (ed.), *Chartist Studies* (London, 1959).
2. *The Brontës: Their Lives, Friendships and Correspondence*, ed. Wise and Symington, vol. II, pp. 202–3.
3. Ibid., p. 203.
4. *The Making of the English Working Class* (Harmondsworth, 1970), p. 613.
5. *The Life of Charlotte Brontë*, ed. Ward and Shorter, p. 53.
6. *Shirley*, ed. Ward and Shorter, ch. 19., p. 345.
7. Ch. 19, p. 345.
8. Ch. 19, p. 352.
9. Ch. 19, p. 353.
10. Ch. 19, p. 355.
11. Ch. 8, p. 136.
12. Ch. 2, p. 28.
13. Ch. 12, p. 226.
14. See Ward and Wilson (eds.), *Land and Industry*, p. 12.
15. Ch. 14, p. 212.
16. Ch. 21, p. 379.
17. Ch. 21, p. 377.
18. See G. D. H. Cole and R. Postgate, *The Common People, 1746–1946* (London, 1946) p. 187, and P. Gregg, *A Social and Economic History of Britain* (London, 1950) p. 50, 1946 ed.
19. Ch. 11, p. 209.
20. Ch. 31, p. 569.
21. Ch. 18, p. 336.
22. Ch. 11, p. 201.
23. Ch. 4, p. 44.
24. Ch. 4, p. 48.
25. Ch. 21, p. 379.
26. Ch. 13, p. 248.
27. Ch. 12, p. 226.
28. Ch. 21, p. 387.
29. Ch. 11, p. 203.
30. Ch. 10, p. 172.
31. Ch. 20, p. 364.
32. Ch. 7, pp. 106–7.
33. Ch. 21, p. 385.

34. Ch. 11, p. 192.
35. Ch. 37, p. 660.
36. Ch. 18, pp. 328–9.
37. Ch. 31, pp. 564–5.

38. Ch. 29, pp. 536–7.
39. Ch. 31, pp. 570–1.
40. Ch. 35, p. 623.
41. Ch. 16, p. 308.

## Chapter 4: Villette

1. *Jane Eyre*, Ch. 4, p. 26.
2. Ch. 10, p. 100.
3. Ch. 35, p. 513.
4. *Villette*, ed. Ward and Shorter, ch. 5, p. 47.
5. Ch. 7, pp. 71–2.
6. Ch. 3, p. 21.
7. Ch. 2, p. 9.
8. Ch. 3, p. 33.
9. Ch. 1, p. 2.
10. Ch. 4, p. 39.
11. Ch. 4, pp. 39–40.
12. Ch. 6, p. 56.
13. Ch. 5, p. 51.
14. Ch. 9, p. 94.
15. Ch. 5, p. 50.
16. Ch. 31, p. 431.
17. Ch. 8, p. 78.
18. Ch. 8, p. 82.
19. Ch. 8, p. 82.
20. Ch. 8, p. 82.

21. Ch. 8, p. 83.
22. Ch. 8, p. 84.
23. Ch. 8, p. 84.
24. *The Professor*, ch. 25, p. 271.
25. *Villette*, ch. 36, p. 504.
26. Ch. 27, p. 371.
27. Ch. 27, p. 372.
28. Ch. 31, p, 433.
29. Ch. 31, p. 433.
30. Ch. 29, p. 406.
31. Ch. 17, p. 212.
32. Ch. 20, p. 258.
33. Ch. 17, p. 226.
34. Ch. 22, p. 296.
35. Ch. 27, p. 379.
36. Ch. 27, p. 380.
37. Ch. 27, p. 376.
38. Ch. 1, p. 1.
39. Ch. 27, p. 369.
40. Ch. 23, p. 306.
41. Ch. 2, p. 11.

## Chapter 5: The Structure of Charlotte Brontë's Fiction

1. *Shirley*, Ch. 29, pp. 537–8.
2. Ch. 1, p. 1.
3. Ch. 37, p. 651.
4. *Villette*, Ch. 12, pp. 126–7.

5. Ch. 15, p. 187.
6. Ch. 6, pp. 62–3.
7. Ch. 42, pp. 593–4.

## Chapter 6: Wuthering Heights

1. See Lukács, *The Historical Novel*, esp. chs. 1–2.
2. Quoted by J. Hillis Miller, *The Disappearance of God* (Cambridge, Mass., 1963) p. 163.
3. Quoted by Leavis, *Lectures in America*, p. 127.
4. *Wuthering Heights*, ed. Ward and Shorter, ch. 14, p. 155.

5. Ch. 15, p. 168.
6. Ch. 4, p. 36.
7. Ch. 12, p. 130.
8. Leavis, p. 99.
9. Ch. 8, p. 66.
10. *Brontë Society Transactions*, no. 78 (1968).
11. *Modern Quarterly Miscellany*, no. 1 (1947).

12. *English Landed Society in the Nineteenth Century*, p. 233.

13. Ch. 32, pp. 319–20.

## Chapter 7: Anne Brontë

1. *Agnes Grey*, ed. Ward and Shorter, ch. 7, p. 418.
2. Ch. 1, p. 35.
3. Ch. 11, p. 442.
4. Ch. 11, p. 442.
5. *The Tenant of Wildfell Hall*, ed. Ward and Shorter, ch. 1, p. 2.
6. Ch. 1, p. 5.
7. Ch. 3, p. 27.
8. Ch. 3, p. 22.
9. Ch. 2, p. 13.
10. Winnifrith, *The Brontës and their Background*, p. 186.
11. Ch. 25, p. 221.
12. Ch. 45, p. 403.
13. Ch. 7, p. 415.

# Index